100 BRACHOS

Counting Your Blessings
100 Times A Day

By Rabbi Moshe Goldberger

The Judaica Press, Inc.

ISBN 1-880582-56-2

THE JUDAICA PRESS, INC.
123 Ditmas Avenue, Brooklyn, New York 11218
718-972-6200 • 800-972-6201
info@judaicapress.com • www.judaicapress.com

Manufactured in the United States of America

ספר זה

מוקדש לעילוי נשמת

האשה החשובה
רחל בת אברהם
זכרונה לברכה
טרענק

ת.נ.צ.ב.ה

מהמשפחה

This *sefer* is dedicated by the Trenk families of
Staten Island, Boro Park, Spring Valley, and Toronto
as a *zichron netzach*, to the memory of a great *neshama*,
a wonderful woman, whom we will never forget.

Rachel Trenk, a"h
bas Reb Avraham Rosenthal, shlita

We will never forget her perennial smile,
Her love of *chessed*, her selfless giving to all.
Her pride in *tznius*, her kind and encouraging words.
Her daily "Have a good day" in the morning, and
Her daily "How was your day?" in the evening.
Her *chochmas noshim*, her intelligence, not flaunting it, never condescending,
Never imposing, always uplifting. Her level-headed thinking, her wise advice,
Her mediation of discord, her love and caring for people,
For her family, for her students, her *shmiras haloshon*, guarding her tongue,
Her self control, her acceptance of others' faults.
Her supreme devotion to her husband and children.
Her acceptance of extra chores to enable her husband to learn and teach Torah,
Her going the extra mile for people, which was her trademark.
Her *simchas hachaim*, her love and appreciation of life,
Her golden *middos tovos* and sterling character.

Rachel was a walking *kiddush Hashem*. She left an imprint on all who met her.
She was a *kiddush Hashem* in her acceptance of suffering. Her never-ending
hope and cheerfulness amazed and strengthened all her visitors, doctors, and
nurses who saw her. Rachel made a *kiddush Hashem* with the way she lived an
observant Jewish life and with her faithful acceptance of her illness.

Rachel's life is eternal. Rachel's memory is eternal.
Her *neshama* surely rests with all the righteous in Gan Eden.

T'HI NISHMASA TZRURA BITZROR HACHAIM, AMEN.

Table of Contents

100 Blessings a Day

*I*magine the benefits we would gain, if, every day, 100 times a day, we recited all our blessings with feeling and authentically focused on Hashem's kindness! We could not help but feel exuberant and enjoy life more by being conscious and appreciative of all that we are blessed with.

Think of at least 100 acts of kindness that Hashem does for us each and every day; this is bound to dispel any cloud of melancholy.

Most of the 100 blessings listed here are said

every day in our normal activities. However, we have to learn to concentrate on what we are saying. With focus, we will learn how to tap into a never-ending spring of happiness.

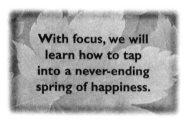

With focus, we will learn how to tap into a never-ending spring of happiness.

Imagine if, for the next 100 days, we choose one blessing a day to pay particular attention to, and we consider to Whom we are saying the blessing, and how fortunate we are to have this astounding blessing.

On day two we can select a second blessing, the next day a third, etc. After 100 days we will have reached our goal of saying all 100 blessings with greater concentration and deeper joy!

It's almost guaranteed that doing this is transformative. We will become imbued with gratitude and happiness, and fall in love with Hashem, Who is doing so much for us. This process is called "repentance out of love," returning to Hashem through *simcha*, by concentrating on all the blessings we are showered with more than 100 times a day (*Chovos Halevovos*).

Every bracha obligates us to make ourselves aware of the benefits we enjoy and accustoms us to feeling gratitude for every additional advantage we enjoy daily. When eating a fruit, for example, we should think of Who created the tree and the fruit, and this will bring us to a constant awareness of Hashem. As the posuk says: "I shall sing to Hashem in my lifetime; I shall sing as long as I exist" (*Tehillim* 145:2).

As we can see from this posuk in *Tehillim*, the purpose of our lives is to utilize being alive to engender feelings of gratitude to Hashem, our Creator and Provider. "The dead do not praise Hashem" (*Tehillim* 115:17) of their own free will. The more we sing to Hashem while we are alive, the greater our eternal reward will be for fulfilling our purpose in this world.

How to Say a Bracha

*H*ashem *created us and provides us with* a world chock-full of bounty. Hashem expects payment for each and every item He created. Even if you own the field, you must still pay for eating a fruit by expressing thanks for the benefit that you are receiving from Hashem.

In *Hilchos Brachos* (1:4), the Rambam notes that there are three types of brachos:

1. Brachos for the pleasure one enjoys from food or drink;

2. Brachos for the performance of a mitzvah; and

3. Brachos of thanks, praise, or requests, in order to always remember the Creator.

In all these cases, we have to think before we make any bracha. Just like there are manners or etiquette in everyday life, there is a certain etiquette to making brachos. The *Mishna Berurah*, for instance, cautions that one should not recite a bracha too quickly. Time should be taken to pause and consider the kindness of Hashem or the gift of a mitzvah opportunity that one is about to be involved in and say the bracha with sincere concentration (*Mishna Berurah, siman* 5:1).

Some Other Guidelines:

ๆ When saying any bracha, we should keep in mind that we are speaking directly to the Creator and King of the Universe. Therefore, it's clear we should always pray or recite a blessing in a respectful manner.

ๆ We may not recite a bracha while we are busy working (*Shulchan Aruch*, 183:12).

ๆ We should not even do light tasks while saying a bracha (*Mishna Berurah* 191:5).

Why is this halacha taught in two places in *Shulchan Aruch* (in *siman* 183 and 191)? The *Mishna Berurah* (191:6)

> The Rambam codifies the laws of brachos under the heading of *ahava*—love. Every bracha expresses our love of Hashem.

explains that we are first taught not to start the bracha until we finish or interrupt whatever we are doing. Then we are taught not to start any task during the recital of a blessing.

ᑫ It is advisable to say brachos aloud since this inspires us to focus and concentrate with more attention (see *Shulchan Aruch, siman* 61:4).

Thirteen Verses

*S*efer *Olas Tamid* lists thirteen verses one
fulfills each time one says brachos properly:
1. Saying a bracha properly means we are
careful not to mention Hashem's name in vain
(*Shemos* 20:7);

2. When we say a bracha properly, this
acknowledges that we have not forgotten
Hashem (*Devarim* 6:12);

3. The proper saying of a bracha means we
are focusing on and remembering the kindness
that Hashem performs for us (*Devarim* 8:2);

4. Saying a bracha in the proper way signifies that we are remembering Hashem (*Devarim* 8:18);

5. Saying a bracha properly signifies that we are fearing Hashem (*Devarim* 10:20);

6. Saying a bracha properly signifies that we are clinging to Hashem (*Devarim* 10:20);

7. Saying a bracha properly means that we are serving Hashem wholeheartedly (*Devarim* 11:13);

8. Saying a bracha properly signifies that we are serving Hashem with joy and happiness (*Devarim* 28:47);

9. Saying a bracha properly requires that we serve Hashem with a combination of rejoicing and trembling (*Tehillim* 2:11);

10. Saying a bracha properly signifies that we are keeping Hashem in mind always (*Tehillim* 16:8);

11. Saying a bracha properly signifies that we are thanking and blessing Hashem for He is always kind to us (*Tehillim* 100:4);

12. Saying a bracha properly signifies that we are trying to relate to Hashem in all of our ways (*Mishlei* 3:6);

13. Saying a bracha properly signifies that we are blessing the Righteous One (*Mishlei* 10:7).

Count Your Blessings

O ne of the best ways to serve Hashem with joy is to stay focused on one's blessings. This shouldn't be difficult since, in fact, every Jew is required to recite a minimum of 100 blessings every day. This is stated openly as law in the *Shulchan Aruch* (46:3), *Laws of Blessings*: "A person is obligated to make, minimally, one hundred blessings every day." The 100 blessings are to be recited by both males and females, (see *Mishna Berurah* [70:2] and *Aruch Hashulchan* [70:1]).

Reciting at least one hundred blessings a day proclaims a general framework of our appreciation for His bounty to us. If we would itemize all the benefits which we receive from Hashem we could list thousands of them. But it would be impossible for anyone to say a thousand blessings a day. Our Sages have selected one hundred primary blessings for us to focus on.

The *Mishna Berurah* (*Shulchan Aruch* 46:3) lists the blessings we typically make during the course of a day, and surmises that, on an average day, one says about one hundred and eight blessings. One hundred, however, is the *minimum* number of blessings one should say daily.

Imagine pausing every day, one hundred times, to appreciate the good fortune that Hashem is constantly sending your way!

"Hashem, You are showering me with such abundant prosperity! Thank You!" It takes just some focusing and awareness to realize that every person receives countless gifts every day from Hashem. These gifts are right before us; all we have to do is to open our eyes, heart and brain to recognize them, appreciate them and be grateful to Hashem for them.

Saying these blessings is such an important obligation that in *parshas Eikev* (*Devarim* 10:12) it states, "What (מה) does Hashem Your G-d ask of you?" This is the only place in the Torah where we find a summary of all of our obligations to Hashem. In *Mesechta Menachos* (43b) we learn, "Rebbe Meir used to say: A man is obligated to bless 100 (מאה) blessings every day. As it states: What (מה) does Hashem want from you?" The word מה is understood to refer to the number of blessings, i.e., מאה, 100. Rebbe Meir explains that this means that Hashem desires, for our benefit, that we utter 100 blessings every day.

> In order to derive maximum benefits from these blessings, we have to concentrate when we say them.

However, in order to derive maximum benefits from these blessings, we have to concentrate when we say them to become inspired in our service to Hashem with gratitude and love.

The Rambam (*Hilchos Tefillah*, chapter 7) teaches this obligation to recite 100 blessings a day. He notes that if one falls short on any single day, one should make up the difference by eating various foods in order to reach the required daily number of blessings.

King Dovid and 100 Brachos

During the days of Dovid Hamelech, the Jews were confronted with a plague and people perished at an alarming rate. Every day, one hundred Jews died. The Sages investigated with *ruach hakodesh* and realized that the plague was a specific message from Hashem. Hence, the sages decreed that every Jew should recite one hundred heartfelt blessings daily to express their appreciation for being alive. Once this was implemented, people stopped dying (*Tur,* ch. 46, quoting Rav Netrunoi Gaon).

This is the original source of the 100 blessings a day. Hopefully, this will motivate us to recite the blessings with both concentration and enthusiasm by acknowledging the protective power blessings have. Hashem deals with us measure for measure; when we appreciate the details of the life He is bestowing on us, we justify its continuation.

Count Your Blessings Chart

Based on the Mishna Berurah (46:14)

Hamapil	1 bracha
Morning	18 brachos
For Torah	3 brachos
Tzitzis & Tefillin	3 brachos
During the prayers	10 brachos
Shemoneh Esrei (3×19)	57 brachos
Two meals with bentching	12 brachos
Total	**104 brachos**

Misc. Brachos:
- For snacks of drinks or fruit, etc.
- For caring for the body.

Who is Wealthy?

oncentrating on the content of these 100 blessings while saying them will generate enormous simcha within us. Why? We learn: "Who is a wealthy person? One who rejoices with one's portion" (*Avos* 4:1).

Once these blessings become an integral part of our days, they will change our awareness of our lives. For example, one of the hundred blessings is for our eyes—one of the grandest gift we have! Is it not incumbent upon us to thank Hashem for the gift of sight? Why wait for a vision problem, G-d forbid, before we begin to appreciate our eyes? Hashem has provided us with two eyes, windows to the astonishing beauty of the world! Hashem gave us eyes which are priceless and irreplaceable!

> Focusing on our many blessings will inspire us to be content, even happy, all the time.

Once we focus on thanking Hashem for each blessing, we will begin to appreciate the gifts the Master of the Universe has given us and keeps on providing. Thus, we will be inspired to develop a general overall, ongoing, cheerful attitude.

Acknowledging and focusing on our many blessings — our abilities to breathe, sing, walk, eat, think, etc. — will inspire us to be content, even happy all the time. Why pay a psychiatrist $200 an hour to treat depression, when we can implement Hashem's antidote for depression? Hashem bestows upon us at least 100 fabulous blessings every day. The last teaching in *Pirkei Avos* (6:12) states that everything that Hashem created in His universe was intended only to bring honor to Him. A bracha fulfills this purpose!

The *Sefer Kuzari* (3:15-17) explains how saying brachos properly can develop into a lifetime career of singing to Hashem and enjoying the pleasures of Hashem's bounty:

"One's pleasure is enhanced by the obligation to say a blessing for everything one enjoys and for all that occurs in one's life. Shouldn't one gain more pleasure than animals do from that which one partakes? One has the option to feel conscious enjoyment...One has the capacity to appreciate and enjoy...By preparing for [our enjoyment] with thought and a heartfelt bracha one increases one's enjoyment. The more attention and devotion, the more pleasure and gratitude toward the Giver."

Thanking Hashem for Being Spared

s we study the system of brachos our Sages have instituted, we should note their specific method of arousing our attention and appreciation.

In the Asher Yatzar blessing, which we say throughout the day — whenever we care for our bodily needs — we describe what would happen if our physical system failed to function properly. This method, of imagining the body's failure to function, prompts us to be sincerely grateful for the efficiency with which our body functions. When we thank Hashem, we are also acknowledging the alternative that could have been our lot. We are then more readily able to appreciate that which we have and to thank Hashem for these gifts wholeheartedly.

> **When we thank Hashem, we are also acknowledging the alternative that could have been our lot.**

When we thank Hashem for our eyesight, for example, we consider (in the blessing) the plight of someone who is blind. By this means, we are motivated to reflect on our good fortune for having the gift of sight and on the enormous debt of gratitude we owe Hashem. We should continually attempt to experience some of the ecstasy experienced by a blind person who, after years of sightlessness, regains his sight. For many weeks afterward, he feasts his eyes on every single item in his surroundings, delirious with the happiness of this blessed gift.

Similarly, when we come upon a handicapped person in a wheelchair, we must consider this as a message from G-d—a reminder of His gifts of mobility to us.

When saying the blessing... "Who establishes a man's footsteps," we should attempt to recapture some of the gratitude felt when viewing someone less fortunate.

In G-d's world there are *no* accidents. When we

encounter someone less fortunate than we are, Hashem is sending us—at the very least—an opportunity to appreciate what we have and the chance to thank Him for it. When witnessing others' misfortunes, it is wise to learn gratitude to Hashem and thereby be spared the necessity of personal experience. Even studying a list of illnesses that we are *not* plagued with should elicit in us a permanent glow of gratitude to Hashem for being spared!

When one fears one has contracted a debilitating illness, *chas veshalom*, but is then subsequently informed by a physician that one's fears are groundless, *boruch Hashem*, one is filled with powerful feelings of joy and gratitude. These feelings should be preserved and one should remain forever grateful to Hashem for having been saved.

Just as people who have been cured of a serious disease are joyous, so too, those of us who have been spared from illness should sing and dance all our days in appreciation and gratitude. May we merit to enjoy "The sound of singing and salvation in the tents of the righteous" (*Tehillim* 118:15) in our homes.

Blessings that Include Prayers

*T*he third category of blessings we explained above in Chapter Two refers to blessings which include prayer requests from Hashem, such as in the Shemoneh Esrei. These blessings require a special focus, a particular way of concentrating.

The Talmud and our Sages advise:

"During prayer, one should direct one's gaze downward and one's heart upward..." (*Yevamos* 105b).

This interesting Talmudic dictum is quoted by

the Rif in the fifth perek of Brachos and explained by Rabbeinu Yonah:

"...'Heart upward' refers to the objective of imagining that one is standing in Heaven. This includes removing the feelings towards physical pleasures and earthly desires from one's heart and elevating oneself."

In modern terminology this means: When we are prepared to speak to G-d in prayer, Hashem says, "OK, but let's meet at My office in Heaven!"

> **When we are prepared to speak to Hashem in prayer, Hashem says, "OK, but let's meet at My office in Heaven!"**

Rabbeinu Yonah continues: "...'Eyes downward' refers to an additional objective. After climbing to the Heavens, one should imagine that one is standing in the Bais HaMikdash on this earth, humble oneself and cause one's prayers to be more acceptable to the Omnipresent One."

Many of the 100 blessings we say daily include prayers to Hashem which have the added significance of asking Hashem to help us gain such benefits as intellect, health, prosperity....

The *Kuzari* (3:5) teaches: "The times of prayer should be the heart of one's day..." Just as the three meals we eat daily sustain our physical needs, so too do our prayer times serve as the spiritual meals that nourish us and keep us going throughout the day.

Prayer is a skillful art which takes practice and training. Before we begin the standing prayer of Shemoneh Esrei in which we converse directly with Hashem, we say a prayer before the prayer: "ה' שפתי תפתח, ופי יגיד תהלתך, Hashem, open up my lips, and enable my mouth to declare Your praise."

Before we even begin to say the Shemoneh Esrei, we plead that Hashem assist us in:

☙ Opening our lips and mouths — which means providing us with the physical abilities, health, and power with which to pray, and

☙ Relating His praise! We should have the sense to appreciate Hashem and praise Him wholeheartedly, sincerely, energetically, and enthusiastically.

Now that we have studied a bit about the significance of reciting blessings for 100 daily gifts, we'll study each bracha to learn how to rejoice — and how to imagine our life without our blessings.

The 100 Brachos

*N*ow that we've studied some of the reasons we should be thankful, and we've looked at the attitude and ideal intentions of blessings and prayer, we are ready to focus on each of the 100 brachos we say daily. In the following pages you'll find each bracha with some comments. You're not expected to read the entire book at once. We suggest that you study one bracha daily for 100 days to help deepen your understanding and appreciation of our daily 100 brachos.

Bracha #1
The Gift of Sleep

בָּרוּךְ אַתָּה ה׳ אֱלֹקֵינוּ מֶלֶךְ הָעוֹלָם, הַמַּפִּיל חֶבְלֵי שֵׁנָה עַל עֵינָי...

"Blessed are You, Eternal Master, our G-d, King of the universe,
Who causes the fetters of sleep to fall on my eyes...."

The blessing we say before going to sleep for the night is counted as our first blessing of the day, for we start each new day the night before, as it says in the *Chumash,* "It was evening and it was morning, one day" (*Bereishis* 1:5). The brachos in Maariv are not counted as the first brachos because they correspond to the offerings at the Bais HaMikdash where we consider the day before the night.

"This world is a hallway before the World to Come, prepare yourself to enter the palace" (*Avos* 4). Darkness precedes light symbolizing that while we are alive our life is a form of concealment, preceding the light of the Afterlife. We go to sleep with the intention of recharging our batteries so that we can serve Hashem in the morning. The blessing said before we go to sleep is a blessing for the gift of sleep. If you have never thanked Hashem for the gift of sleep, you owe Hashem a tremendous debt of gratitude. Sleep allows one to lay down one's body and allow one's mind to go into a slumber-mode, which is *geshmack* (pleasurable and perfect). *Nebach* (what a tragedy), when someone has insomnia. One who has suffered even once from this difficulty learns how invaluable a good night's sleep is.

The vast majority of people fall asleep easily. What is more, most of us are privileged to sleep on soft, comfortable materials that Hashem has provided, such as the luxury to place our head on a soft pillow, our body on a comfortable bed and soft linens.

The Torah tells us that Yaakov *Avinu* once went to sleep with only a rock for a pillow (*Bereishis* 28:18). You, however, do not have a boulder for a pillow; you have a soft, perhaps feathery cushion with a soft pillow cover. You place your tired head down upon it and think: "O, Hashem, thank You so much for the soft pillow!" As you fall asleep you muse: "Ah, the *Abishter* provides me with the best of everything."

> The Abishter re-energizes and rejuvenates us, so that when we awake, we are refreshed and full of renewed vigor.

The process of falling asleep is similar to a treatment of anesthesia, but we pay no anesthesiologist. Sleep is transformative. The *Abishter* re-energizes, revitalizes and rejuvenates us, so that when we awake, we are restored and refreshed, full of renewed strength and vigor. This is a *gevaldige* (amazing, fantastic, unbelievable) gift. The *Medrash* (*Eicha* 3:23) illustrates this with an example of someone who stores a precious item for safekeeping and hopes to have it returned in one piece, but would not expect it to be improved. If we owed the guardian of this precious object a lot of money we would understand if they refused to return the item but insisted on holding it as collateral.

When we sleep, we are in Hashem's hands for safekeeping. We hope that we will wake up and that we will be refreshed and renewed. Both of these are gifts that Hashem does *not* owe us. Hashem, grants us a tremendous gift— when we awake in the morning Hashem restores our soul so that we wake with renewed energy.

The Gemara *Brachos* (57b) teaches that "sleep is like one sixtieth of death." Sleep serves as a daily reminder of our inevitable end in this world. One of the benefits of sleep is that it imposes a deadline on our daily activities. This prompts us to include in our blessing before we go to sleep: "Please wake me in the morning; my sleep should not be my demise."

Pirkei D'Rebbe Eliezer (12) lists some of the benefits of sleep: It is like food (sustenance), it is like medicine (healing), it provides life and it provides us with peace of mind.

Blessings Upon Awakening

W*hen we wake up in the morning, our* first act is to wash our hands, and recite a blessing to Hashem.

Bracha #2
The Gift of Hands

בָּרוּךְ אַתָּה ה' אֱלֹקֵינוּ מֶלֶךְ הָעוֹלָם
אֲשֶׁר קִדְּשָׁנוּ בְּמִצְוֹתָיו, וְצִוָּנוּ עַל נְטִילַת יָדָיִם:

"Blessed are You, Eternal Master, our G-d, King of the universe, Who has sanctified us with His commandments, and commanded us regarding the washing of hands."

ক্ষ ক্ষ ক্ষ

Having clean hands after our long sleep decreases the likelihood of being infected by germs. This hygienic practice of washing our hands prevents many illnesses. The Torah desires cleanliness for our health and benefit and the Sages teach us the necessity of coupling our washing in the morning with a blessing as a preparation for prayer. It is also a process of sanctification: A kohen would wash his hands at the Mikdash before beginning to serve (*Mishna Berurah, Orach Chayim* 4:1).

As we pour the water over our hands, we can thank *HaKadosh Boruch Hu* for giving us hands, water and a cup! We probably have a sink faucet which allows us to get the water without having to make a trip to a well. These are all great blessings — including the fact that you were blessed with hands. Your hands are a wonderful gift!

While washing, it's a good time to consider that we have ten fingers. Look at them now. The five on one hand are all of a different size, each one suited to specific tasks. How many fingers are used for writing? What about for using a push-button phone? People tend to get more excited over their new cell phones than over the miracle of their hands!

We should think about our hands and thank Hashem for them at least five times a day.

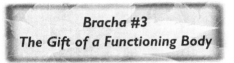

Bracha #3
The Gift of a Functioning Body

בָּרוּךְ אַתָּה ה' אֱלֹקֵינוּ מֶלֶךְ הָעוֹלָם, אֲשֶׁר יָצַר אֶת הָאָדָם בְּחָכְמָה.

"Blessed are You, Eternal Master, our G-d, King of the universe, Who formed man with wisdom…"

This blessing is recited many times a day, whenever one has to urinate or relieve oneself. An entire book can be written on this blessing alone.

Hashem has presented most of us with a fully functioning, billion dollar body. Without any work on our part, our body acts as a perfect machine, expelling waste and retaining the nutrients we need for our continued well-being. There are people plagued with difficulty in eliminating. There are those who must be strapped for hours to a dialysis machine, twice a week. Fortunately, Hashem has spared most of us from these terrible ailments. We owe a tremendous debt of gratitude to the Holy One, Blessed be He, when our body functions so perfectly and efficiently.

a. "Who has formed a person with wisdom…"

(This blessing is explained in detail in *Shulchan Aruch, Orach Chayim* 6). Our physical body is a universe full of miraculous wonders. We are required to admire and thank Hashem for this marvelous machine which Hashem has created and loaned to us. Each of the human body's components is more complicated than any complex machine; it has more things running in sync than a huge skyscraper building with all of its details of steel framework, masonry, plumbing, ventilation, lighting, hardware, fixtures and furniture.

One aspect of this wonderful creation is that the human body is similar to a balloon full of air, which deflates immediately if even a tiny hole punctures it. Nevertheless, although the human body is full of openings, a human's ability to survive is not harmed by them.

b. "and created within him many openings…"

"And created within him many openings (mouth, nose, ears and the openings that emit the bodily wastes), and many hollow organs (heart, stomach, intestines…) if one of them would be opened (at the wrong time) or if one of them would be blocked (when it should be open), it would be impossible to exist." While a fetus is developing in its mother's womb its mouth is non-functional. However, as soon as a baby emerges from the womb the mouth begins to function. Similarly, throughout one's life one's many orifices must function constantly in an extremely specific fashion for a person to be healthy.

The kidneys circulate blood to keep it clean. 2,000 pounds of blood pass daily through 280 miles of small tubes in the kidneys.

We should take time to consider the opening and closing of each of our many organs, and thank Hashem for our mouth, heart, stomach, lungs, pancreas, liver, kidneys, etc.

c. "Thank You, Hashem, the Healer of all flesh..."

The emission of bodily wastes is crucial to a human's survival. This process is compared to a complicated surgical operation that Hashem has built into our body as an automatic system.

d. "Who works wondrously."

This refers to the intricate system through which nutrients are separated from the food we eat. An exact amount of each specific nutrient is delivered to each part of the body, while the unwanted wastes are rejected and expelled in two separate systems which exist for liquid and solid wastes.

In addition, we marvel over the fact that the physical maintenance of the body, by means of the proper physical care, suffices to somehow keep the soul attached to the body.

This blessing "who works wondrously" is a general thanks to Hashem for all of the wonders of the human body and for our over-all physical health.

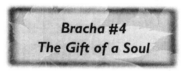

Bracha #4
The Gift of a Soul

אֱלֹקַי, נְשָׁמָה שֶׁנָּתַתָּ בִּי טְהוֹרָה הִיא...

"My G-d, the soul You have placed in me is pure..."

❧ ❧ ❧

The soul within us is a portion from Hashem. We contain a Divine core of spiritual life that makes us like Hashem. The Gemara (*Brachos* 10a) teaches that there are five similarities between Hashem and our essential *neshama*:

1. Hashem fills the universe; the *neshama* fills our body.

2. Both Hashem and the *neshama* see all, but cannot be seen by humans.

3. Hashem sustains all; the *neshama* sustains the body.

4. Both Hashem and our *neshama* are pure.

5. Both Hashem and our *neshama* reside in hidden chambers.

There is no limit to the miraculous power of the soul that is contained in our bodies.

"Beloved is man who was created in the image of Hashem" (*Avos* 3:14).

"The soul that You gave me is pure…"

Every morning we thank G-d for restoring our soul to our body. Whenever the Creator wakes a person, it is a kindness that parallels the revival of the dead. We not only regain our consciousness and our ability to move, but we are like someone who has actually been reborn, with a renewed body and mind. Every day we thank Hashem for this process and for the intimation it provides concerning the future revival of the dead (*techiyas hameisim*), which will be an eternal existence of happiness.

Why are we in this world? The answer, which is both simple and powerful, can be found in the following posuk: "Happy is the heart of those who seek Hashem" (*Tehillim* 105:3). Our happiness in life depends mainly on knowing what we are here for. By focusing clearly on striving to come closer to Hashem we gain the intense satisfaction of utilizing our lives fully. This enables us to sense a foretaste of the ecstasy of the Afterlife where we will enjoy the splendor of Hashem's presence (*Brachos* 17a).

The human soul is unfathomable, since it comes from the Creator and reflects His infinite greatness. In *Bereishis*, in the section concerning the creation of Adam, we find, "He blew into his nostrils the breath of life" (*Bereishis* 2:7). "One who blows, blows of himself" (*Ramban*). Hashem blew a portion of Himself into humans; thus each of us contains a spark of the Divine.

We must impress upon ourselves how miraculous and valuable is every human being that Hashem has created; a testimony to the unlimited greatness of the Creator. This bracha surely puts a huge smile on our faces as we realize the potential greatness with which Hashem has endowed us.

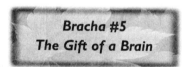

Bracha #5
The Gift of a Brain

בָּרוּךְ אַתָּה ה' אֱלֹקֵינוּ מֶלֶךְ הָעוֹלָם, אֲשֶׁר נָתַן
לַשֶּׂכְוִי בִינָה, לְהַבְחִין בֵּין יוֹם וּבֵין לַיְלָה:

"Blessed are You, Eternal Master, our G-d, King of the universe, Who has given understanding to the mind to distinguish between day and night."

ଈ ଈ ଈ

Most of us are blessed with the possession of an incredible brain that, as we grow, is filled with wisdom, common sense, personality, an ability to understand, perceive, react, process information, etc. This is all an amazing gift from Hashem. The mind has greater complexity than any computer in the world. The human mind has invented computers; however, a computer cannot create a mind. Hashem gave us our mind to serve as the command center of our being.

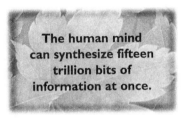

The human mind can synthesize fifteen trillion bits of information at once.

Our Sages teach us how to thank Hashem. Instead of merely generalizing, we focus on one of the first benefits we gain every morning from our mind. The word שכוי, which our sages selected for the word "mind," has two interpretations. Both are related to the topic at hand.

In the language of Tanach, the heart is called שכוי. The heart is the seat of understanding because it registers a person's emotional involvement in an issue. When a person sees the daylight, his or her heart gets excited for a new day of life. The rooster also senses the difference between day and night, and whoever sleeps in the vicinity of a rooster will be aware of the rooster's announcement of early morning. Thus our sages connected the two (*Mishnah Berura* 46:4).

Hashem gave the rooster the ability to sense the approach of day and to announce this news just before daybreak, as an alarm clock would arouse one at a set time. Both a rooster and an alarm clock are useful devices, for which we must be grateful to Hashem. Imagine if you had no way of knowing or arranging for yourself to wake up at a certain time!

We also thank Hashem — for the invention of the mechanical rooster — the alarm clock which serves as a tool to assist the mind and the heart to wake up at a designated time.

We correlate the rooster with the alarm, and thank Hashem for supplying us with a creature/machine geared to recognize the difference between day and night. Without all of the blessings of intelligence, a person's life would be severely limited. We therefore begin this list of brachos with thanks for our mind; we then proceed to thank Hashem for our identity.

To better understand this connection to the rooster, there's an elucidating *Gemara* in *Mesechta Beitzah* (25b).

"There are three bold creations: the Jewish nation amongst the other nations; the dog amongst animals; and the rooster amongst the fowl."

Why are the dog and the rooster considered unique?

The dog excels in the quality of loyalty to its master; a rooster senses the approach of day and announces it loudly, even though the sky is still dark. Jews are compared to both of these creatures. We are similar to a dog because, even in exile, we always remain loyal to Hashem. We are similar to a rooster because, although the world at large is wrapped in the darkness of materialism, we continue to proclaim the truths of the Torah.

We proclaim that this world is not a place to sleep away one's life; we need to achieve in Torah and mitzvos and dispel the darkness (*Sing, You Righteous*, Rabbi Avigdor Miller, pg. 267).

Both our brain and a rooster have the same function — to alert us to the change of time and to the need to rise and shine in Hashem's service.

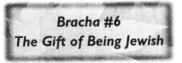

Bracha #6
The Gift of Being Jewish

בָּרוּךְ אַתָּה ה' אֱלֹקֵינוּ מֶלֶךְ הָעוֹלָם, שֶׁלֹּא עֲשַׂנִי גּוֹי:

"Blessed are You, Eternal Master, our G-d, King of the universe, Who did not make me a Goy..."

What an incredible amount of gratitude we owe *HaKadosh Boruch Hu* for making us Jewish. Not only are we created in Hashem's image, but we possess a Jewish soul, which makes us Hashem's chosen ones: His children. He has not created us as gentiles. We are grateful that we are members of the nation chosen by G-d to receive the Torah with its 613 Divine commandments. Each mitzvah is a price-less gift from the Creator for which we must be eternally grateful.

The *Aleinu* prayer is recited three times daily to thank the One Who created us in a distinctive, unique way, worthy of being chosen to become His people forever.

It is written in *Aleinu*: "It is incumbent on us to praise the Master of everything…He did not make us like the nations of the lands…like the families of the Earth, He did not make…our lot like that of their multitude" (*Aleinu*).

In *Avos* (3:14) it says: "Beloved is Yisroel for they are the children of Hashem."

A Jew differs from the peoples of other nations in many ways. The *Gemara Yevamos* (79a), for example, states that a Jew is unique in three ways:

"A Jew is merciful, modest and kindly." Although these traits are not always evident in Jews who neglect to follow the Torah properly, these traits are still embedded in the core of their personality. All human beings were created in Hashem's image, but only Jews are considered Hashem's children (*Avos* 3).

Hashem declares: "This nation I have created for Me, they should relate My praise" (*Yeshaya* 43:21). This verse, by the way, teaches the purpose of this book: to learn how to praise Hashem in one hundred ways. Our mission and purpose in this world should be to praise Hashem for all that He has done and continues to do for us.

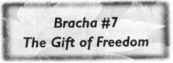

**Bracha #7
The Gift of Freedom**

בָּרוּךְ אַתָּה ה' אֱלֹקֵינוּ מֶלֶךְ הָעוֹלָם, שֶׁלֹּא עָשַׂנִי עָבֶד:

"Blessed are You, Eternal Master, our G-d, King of the universe, Who did not make me a slave."

✥ ✥ ✥

Most Jews today are fortunate not to be enslaved. We are not subjugated to others. We are free, living in a free country, no longer in Egypt or in any of the other lands throughout history where Jews were, in various degrees, once enslaved.

However, even slaves possess a certain amount of free choice, at the very least in how they choose to use their mind. However, one who is not a slave has more freedom of choice. Hashem presents us with a variety of life opportunities we can take advantage of, but the first step is to feel grateful for having any options at all and for understanding what a gift this is.

Our freedom permits us to serve Hashem and meet our obligations to keep all of the Torah's commandments. Hashem redeemed the Jews from Egypt for a specific purpose, as it says: "Send forth my people so that they should serve Me" (*Shemos* 10:3). Hashem freed us from the back-breaking slave labor in Egypt and He elevated us for all time to be His chosen nation. A slave does not own anything, as we learn—"whatever he acquires, belongs to his master" (*Pesachim* 88b). We thank Hashem for freeing us and enabling us to serve Him.

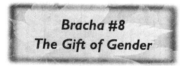

Bracha #8
The Gift of Gender

בָּרוּךְ אַתָּה ה׳ אֱלֹקֵינוּ מֶלֶךְ הָעוֹלָם, שֶׁלֹּא עָשַׂנִי אִשָּׁה:

(Males): "Blessed are You, Eternal Master, our G-d, King of the universe, Who did not make me a woman."

בָּרוּךְ אַתָּה ה׳ אֱלֹקֵינוּ מֶלֶךְ הָעוֹלָם, שֶׁעָשַׂנִי כִּרְצוֹנוֹ:

(Females): "Blessed are You, Eternal Master, our G-d, King of the universe, Who made me according to His Will."

There is one blessing for a male, and another blessing for a female. Either way, *HaKadosh Boruch Hu* gave each of us exactly what *we* need to achieve perfection in this world. Whether we are female or male, Hashem has designed *us* to perfection, furnishing us with the accouterments, abilities and potential, the medium with which to achieve perfection. Hashem and the whole world awaits that special contribution each of us was created to make. But before we can make this contribution, we must realize and accept that Hashem made us who we are, for our benefit, and for the benefit of the world.

A male thanks Hashem for not being made a female. Males express gratitude to G-d for their additional mitzvos, which are not incumbent upon women (generally mitzvos dependent on a time factor). A female thanks Hashem for being made a female, according to His will. Women also say the bracha for not being made a gentile or a slave. Men and women are similar to kohanim, leviim and yisroelim: each group has its specific function in serving Hashem.

Females thank Hashem for their unique biological ability to be mothers, for which they were specifically created, and for the many mitzvos they are obligated to fulfill. Their satisfaction and happiness is derived from different areas of focus than that of men, for they were created by Hashem for specific purposes (*Bereishis* 2:18). All people are obligated to acknowledge their unique potential daily and determine to use their vast powers to accomplish the goals Hashem intended for them to achieve.

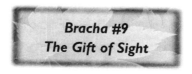

Bracha #9
The Gift of Sight

בָּרוּךְ אַתָּה ה׳ אֱלֹקֵינוּ מֶלֶךְ הָעוֹלָם, פּוֹקֵחַ עִוְרִים:

"Blessed are You, Eternal Master, our G-d, King of the universe, Who opens the eyes of the blind."

≪ ≪ ≪

Most of us have two eyes which work quite miraculously! We thank Hashem daily for the blessing of sight, by means of a pair of the most perfect cameras in existence.

Not long ago there lived a man in France whose entire body was paralyzed. Only one small part of his body was able to move: his left eyelid. With the help of an assistant, he was able to communicate. The assistant would point to letters on an alphabet board and the man would wink his left eyelid when the assistant pointed to the right letter. The assistant would then jot down that letter. Through this laborious process, the man managed to assemble words and sentences. Eventually, through this tedious method, he wrote an entire book by means of his left eyelid alone. As you might well imagine, it took him a long time; however, he persevered. It was published and within a few days, 25,000 copies were sold! The book was that good. In his book, he communicated his deep appreciation for life and his sense of gratitude for being able to move his left eyelid.

He noted that since it took him so long to write each line of the book, he had that much more time to contemplate the message he wished to communicate. He was able to edit everything as he went along so that the finished product was superb. This is an astonishing lesson of how a positive perspective can change even impossible predicaments.

> **The human eye can discriminate among nearly eight million gradations of color.**

Imagine how easy this man would think it is to write a book if you have two eyelids, a left and right one! And imagine how easy he would think it was if one had two hands—and perhaps even a computer! We have so many privileges. Not only do we possess fully functioning eyelids, but also eyelashes, pupils, corneas, irises, peripheral and color vision! When we focus on our miraculous bodies and how they function, we become privy to its beauty. When you say this bracha, revel and rejoice with your eyes. Imagine your predicament without them!

The ability to see is an invaluable gift for which we must thank Hashem. We must consider this gift in detail and continually be grateful for it. Consider the brilliant construction of the bone frame that protrudes and surrounds to protect the eye, the eyelid which automatically rolls down when something approaches the eye, the fluid that bathes and cleanses the eye, the eyebrows and eyelashes. The eye has the ability to adjust for distance and light intensity and many similar benefits.

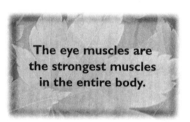

The eye muscles are the strongest muscles in the entire body.

If our eyes are less than perfect and we wear glasses we still must feel grateful. Imagine if there were no available raw materials and inventions necessary to manufacture and process glasses. Hashem created these materials and inspired the inventors of the end product. We should be grateful to Hashem for making these resources available in abundance so that glasses are affordable. And then we should thank Hashem for providing us with the money to pay for our glasses. (We should also thank Hashem for similar, useful inventions that help us view the world based on eye-lens principles—such as cameras, telescopes and microscopes.)

The *Yesod Veshoresh Hoavodah* suggests that one should close one's eyes while saying this bracha and then open them at the conclusion of this bracha, in order to fully enjoy one's eyesight and to intensify one's appreciation and gratitude to Hashem.

We can even take a thank-you-Hashem-for-my-eyes break periodically throughout the day. Begin by practicing right now. Relax, close your eyes, take a deep breath and think: I will open my eyes with Hashem's help and the intention to enjoy the pleasures of the gift of vision Hashem has granted me.

The formula for the blessing is in the present tense— "Hashem is opening the eyes of the blind"—because the gift of sight is an ongoing gift. Every moment we receive benefits and pleasure as we watch our loved ones, and as we take in the blue sky, green grass, a variety of trees, flowers, golden sunshine, and all other colors, shapes and movement that make up the world.

Included in "opening the eyes of the blind" is Hashem's gift of knowledge and understanding ("their eyes were opened" [*Bereishis* 3:7]), without which we would know nothing. The Talmud (*Nedarim* 64b) teaches that blind people are considered as having died in a certain sense, because it often limits their ability to fully interact with others and to participate in life as other people. The gift of sight is like a gift of life. Sight and insight are two of the greatest gifts for which we must always thank Hashem. This in no way insults the blind for they are able to do a tremendous amount and achieve great accomplishments, but still, those who can see must appreciate their gift of sight which offers the opportunity of full and easy participation in society.

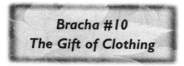

Bracha #10
The Gift of Clothing

בָּרוּךְ אַתָּה ה׳ אֱלֹקֵינוּ מֶלֶךְ הָעוֹלָם, מַלְבִּישׁ עֲרֻמִים:

"Blessed are You, Eternal Master, our G-d,
King of the universe, Who clothes the naked."

Another daily gift we often forget about is the clothing we wear. Hashem provides us with many types of clothing. We must thank Him for the clothing and for all the various benefits of having clothing and wearing them.

Hashem has provided all the materials used to manufacture clothing. This blessing, thanking Hashem for clothing us, should be (mentally) particularized. In the wintertime, we should focus on how thankful we are for our warm wool clothing and a heavy winter coat and various accessories, such as scarves, gloves and boots. In the summertime, we should marvel at our lightweight, cooler clothing. We thank Hashem also for the opportunity on Shabbos and *Yom Tov* to indulge in special, dignified clothing and on special events wear dressy clothing.

We have to remember that the various inventions of cotton, wool, nylon, linen, silk and other materials that are soft and hard, pleasant to the skin and durable, is due to Hashem. We have to remember to include thanks as well for the fabulous invention of buttons and buttonholes, for linings and the convenience of having pockets.

Clothing covers our body to prevent others from seeing what should not be seen. Our physical bodies are covered with modesty to indicate that our soul is the main entity of our being. Clothing also calls attention to that which we would like to be known; namely, clothing expresses our sense of dignity and importance. "Rabbi Yochanon called his garments his honor-givers" (*Shabbos* 133b).

It's interesting to note that the blessing concerning clothing follows the blessing for eyes. (All of the other blessings in this section refer to parts of the body, whereas clothing is an external benefit.) This teaches us an important lesson—

the ability to see, which is a tremendous benefit, can be misused if one uses one's vision to view the wrong things. One who views others who are dressed immodestly teases one's base desires, causing one's temptation to be stirred, and possibly leading to more sins. "Do not stray after your eyes" (*Bamidbar* 15:39). We must use garments to conceal our own nakedness and for others to avoid viewing abominations and indecent exposures and the practices of the wicked. We need to insure that our eyes remain a blessing and we are not tempted to sin. When one's eyes see nakedness it stimulates the mind to think negative thoughts. To prevent this Hashem provides us with eyelids that shut quickly and with clothing to cover and conceal nakedness.

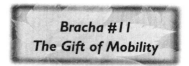

Bracha #11
The Gift of Mobility

בָּרוּךְ אַתָּה ה' אֱלֹקֵינוּ מֶלֶךְ הָעוֹלָם, מַתִּיר אֲסוּרִים:

"Blessed are You, Eternal Master, our G-d,
King of the universe, Who releases the bound."

Hashem grants us the gift of mobility. Most people are able to move around freely; they are not paralyzed or otherwise handicapped. We have to appreciate our ability to move. While asleep, we are immobile. Without Hashem's mercy, we would be unable to move our hand or foot or even raise an eyelid.

This phrase—*"Who releases the bound"*—is significant in that it is actually repeated three times during our prayers:

1. In our morning list of blessings. The *Gemara* (*Brachos* 60b) relates this phrase said in the morning to our ability to sit up in the morning.

2. We also say it in *Pesukei D'zimra* (from *Tehillim* 146:7), where it is part of the verse: "He performs justice for those who are victimized, He gives bread to the hungry, Hashem releases the bound."

It seems odd that Hashem's name is mentioned only in the third part of this verse. Perhaps this indicates that it is the main point of the verse—Hashem's goal is to help release the bound. In order to accomplish that goal, He first punishes the oppressors and feeds the hungry (see *Malbim*'s comment on this verse). This refers to the fact that Hashem has either freed us from prison or He has protected us from being incarcerated and subjected to privation and cruelty in the first place. You may know of someone who did end up in prison for one reason or another. You should pray that Hashem help that person but also be thankful to Hashem that He has been protecting us from such a mishap.

3. In the second blessing of Shemoneh Esrei, we find the statement that "Hashem heals the sick and releases the confined." This alludes to the physical infirmities that Hashem cures us from. One who was sick in bed and is then cured has to realize that his recovery is a result of Hashem having compassion upon him and giving him the health and strength to move. All the more so if Hashem has kept one from becoming ill in the first place.

Thus we should never take these benefits for granted. We owe Hashem thanks and praise for enabling us to sit up, saving us from prison, and preventing us from being ill or disabled.

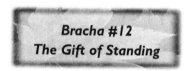

Bracha #12
The Gift of Standing

בָּרוּךְ אַתָּה ה' אֱלֹקֵינוּ מֶלֶךְ הָעוֹלָם, זוֹקֵף כְּפוּפִים:

"Blessed are You, Eternal Master, our G-d,
King of the universe, Who straightens the bent."

Another daily miracle that should make us marvel is our

ability to stand upright. It's often difficult to focus on all of our gifts, but we must study to appreciate every one of them, so that we can thank Hashem for each and every one of the benefits with which He provides us.

We find the phrase "Who straightens the bent" in three places in our prayers, and in each area a different meaning is intended.

1. In the morning blessing, we refer to Hashem's straightening the bent, enabling us to stand up in the morning after being in bed all night;

2. In *Ashrei*, the phrase "He upholds all those who fall and makes erect all those who are bent over," refers to the dignity that Hashem provides people with.

3. The Psalm recited directly after *Ashrei* (*Tehillim* 146) is connected to how Hashem opens the eyes of the blind and makes erect those who are bent over. This includes the lesson that Hashem has arranged for all of our body's components to function in harmony as they interact with each other.

For instance, we benefit from having our eyes positioned near the top of our head so that we can view the world all around from a high perch. Thus we thank Hashem for providing us with eyes and then enabling us to stand erect in order to utilize our eyes for maximum benefit.

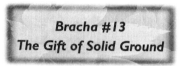

Bracha #13
The Gift of Solid Ground

בָּרוּךְ אַתָּה ה׳ אֱלֹקֵינוּ מֶלֶךְ הָעוֹלָם, רוֹקַע הָאָרֶץ עַל הַמָּיִם:

"Blessed are You, Eternal Master, our G-d, King of the universe,
Who spreads the Earth upon the waters."

❧ ❧ ❧

This blessing refers to the benefit we have to stand on solid ground even though most of the earth is water. In *Bereishis* the Torah spells out how Hashem caused the dry land to appear (1:9). "Upon stepping on the ground in the morning, one should thank Hashem for preparing the Earth upon which one is able to stand" (*Brachos* 60b).

The fact that the earth remains in place is the Creator's provision. "You have set boundaries for the waters so that they do not return to cover the land" (*Tehillim* 104:9).

Why doesn't the land sink into the water? Numerous miracles cause the land upon which we live to remain in its position, above and in the midst of the waters. We must appreciate and thank Hashem daily for this benefit.

Nowadays, we also must appreciate and thank Hashem for the various materials used in cities to afford us smooth pavements and streets.

Bracha #14
Gift of Providing for All Our Needs

בָּרוּךְ אַתָּה ה׳ אֱלֹקֵינוּ מֶלֶךְ הָעוֹלָם, שֶׁעָשָׂה לִי כָּל צָרְכִּי:

"Blessed are You, Eternal Master, our G-d, King of the universe,
Who has supplied me with all my needs."

 formance 🖙 🖙 🖙

The *Gemara* relates this blessing specifically to our shoes. "This blessing is associated with the provision of shoes, which enable a person to get around and take care of his needs" (*Brachos* 60b).

To have shoes is a tremendous *chesed*. Rabbi Avigdor Miller explains in his books how many shoes are constructed with a rubber sole, a comfortable rubber heal, with the tips of shoelaces encased in plastic to make it easier to lace. If the plastic tip falls off the end of the shoelace, it is a struggle to lace up the shoes. We can also buy shoe polish to shine our shoes. Many shoes are made of leather which is durable and comfortable and also dyed with pleasing colors. Many shoes are lined inside for comfort and the bottom is sturdy to protect the feet, yet cushioned to be comfortable. These are all a kindness provided by Hashem. All these different parts of the shoe afford us the maximum benefit and comfort. With shoes, as with everything else, Hashem has "provided us all of our needs."

Our shoes and every one of our other needs, whether made of natural or of man-made materials, are prepared and provided for us by the Creator. He created the materials and then provided the human mind (which is also His creation) with the ideas and inspiration necessary for developing these items.

When we say this blessing, we should appreciate and consider the numerous needs (food, clothing, housing…) Hashem has met for us. Let us also consider that every individual has particular needs — both physical and spiritual — which Hashem has designed for each person's provisions to suit his or her uniqueness (*Alei Shur*). Of all the blessings, this is one of the few in which we say, "Hashem supplies *me*" because our shoe size is unique for us. This represents also the many other items that are custom tailored for each individual.

When we pray for assistance from Hashem we are required to request all that we think we need, because it is Hashem's intention — by not satisfying certain needs — to cause us to need to pray to Him.

Prayer in itself is an urgent need, for it brings us to an awareness of Hashem and to appreciate our many gifts. We must, however, be careful that when we request what we need, we do not complain. Prayer is in no way a session of complaining to Hashem. Rather, in prayer we ask Hashem to continue to provide us with all that we need. Prayer also serves as a daily discipline necessary to help us focus on the fact that all that we have are gifts granted and maintained by Hashem.

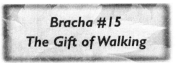

Bracha #15
The Gift of Walking

בָּרוּךְ אַתָּה ה' אֱלֹקֵינוּ מֶלֶךְ הָעוֹלָם, הַמֵּכִין מִצְעֲדֵי גֶבֶר:

"Blessed are You, Eternal Master, our G-d, King of the universe,
Who prepares the steps of a person."

Our ability to walk with our own two feet, without much effort, is a kindness from Hashem. When our feet are functioning we can amble down the avenue, stroll through the street, take our daily constitutional or a weekly jaunt. If we want, we can run a little, jog, trot, sprint or dash. If we're determined, we can run a four-minute mile, walk or run up and down steps. Hashem gave us versatile feet, which are better than the best automobile, because they are a vehicle at our disposal at all times. When we decide to stop walking, there are no complications; we do not have to look for a parking space. We just bend our feet underneath our chair. There is nothing to worry about. The *Abishter* takes care of all of our needs. Walking is a marvelous ability for which we must be eternally grateful to the Creator. We

> Our soles are padded with the toughest skin; ten times thicker than any other skin on our body.

include thanks for our thighs, joints, knees and ankles which harmoniously function as we walk. Even if we think we rarely walk, a person takes an average of 18,000 steps a day, about a distance of eight miles.

We should also consider in this blessing the many additional means of transportation that Hashem has provided for our benefit: bicycles, cars, buses, trains, airplanes, helicopters and boats. Hashem has prepared and prompted humans to develop these for the benefit of humanity.

Bracha #16
The Gift of Strength

בָּרוּךְ אַתָּה ה׳ אֱלֹקֵינוּ מֶלֶךְ הָעוֹלָם, אוֹזֵר יִשְׂרָאֵל בִּגְבוּרָה:

"Blessed are You, Eternal Master, our G-d, King of the universe, Who girds Yisroel with might."

❧ ❧ ❧

Hashem girds and imbues us with strength. *Chazal* tell us that this bracha is said in reference to the habit of wearing a belt (or waistband) (*Brachos* 60b). Rabbi Avigdor Miller (*Awake My Glory*, p. 222) speaks about belt holes. A belt usually has five holes, enabling one to adjust it for the maximum comfort and effectiveness: one hole for before a meal and one hole, when one loosens one's belt, for after a meal. In this way, males do not have to worry about pants being too tight or too loose. One must also recognize the worth of the leather of genuine cowhide, the width of the belt so that it does not cause a welt, the long-lasting and good looking metal buckle. A belt is something to be enjoyed, appreciated and to thank Hashem for.

We thank Hashem specifically for providing us with the means to strengthen ourselves physically and spiritually. In addition, we realize that we would not be able to overcome temptation if Hashem did not help us (*Kiddushin* 30b). Who is the true possessor of *gevura*? "Who is mighty? He who conquers his inclination" (*Avos* 4:1). Hashem does not only provide us with our needs, He always remains at our side to assist us.

Why does this blessing have the word "Yisroel" mentioned specifically? Because a belt has symbolic, spiritual benefits as well as physical benefits. The belt serves to separate between one's heart and one's lower parts (*Brachos* 24b). This reminds us to gird ourselves with added strength to battle the wickedness of the outside world and the temptations of human nature.

Each and every one of these blessings is a reason to be full of *simcha*. We have so far mentioned sixteen blessings, but there are many more. The more we can ruminate about each of these items throughout the day, the more we can fulfill our overall objective of "speaking in all of His wonders" (*Tehillim* 105:2).

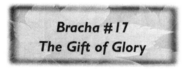

Bracha #17
The Gift of Glory

בָּרוּךְ אַתָּה ה׳ אֱלֹקֵינוּ מֶלֶךְ הָעוֹלָם, עוֹטֵר יִשְׂרָאֵל בְּתִפְאָרָה:

"Blessed are You, Eternal Master, our G-d, King of the universe,
Who crowns Yisroel with glory."

ﻌ ﻌ ﻌ

The Gemara *Brachos* (60b) explains this bracha as referring to a head covering. Males wear hats which cover their head and remind them that Hashem is above them at all times. According to the laws of the Torah (*Kesuvos* 72a), a married woman is also required to cover her head whenever in the presence of men. This demonstrates her loyalty to Hashem. A young girl displays her hair as a sign that she is eligible for marriage (Rabbi Miller, *Awake My Glory*, p. 729).

A hat is a sign of the dignity Hashem bestowed on Jews. It makes one feel taller and more dignified and respected. A Jewish male covers his head at all times to signify his mindfulness of Hashem, as it says, "cover your head so that you will gain the fear of Heaven" (*Shabbos* 156b).

Hats (or yarmulkas) should be considered as if they were royal crowns of glory! And when these hats or coverings are worn, gratitude should be expressed for the comfortable cloth or felt, the fit on our head size, the inside lining, the brim and the pleasing color.

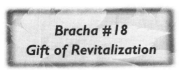

Bracha #18
Gift of Revitalization

בָּרוּךְ אַתָּה ה' אֱלֹקֵינוּ מֶלֶךְ הָעוֹלָם, הַנּוֹתֵן לַיָעֵף כֹּחַ:

"Blessed are You, Eternal Master, our G-d, King of the universe,
Who gives strength to the weary."

❧ ❧ ❧

How does a weary person revitalize oneself? When one

wakes up in the morning, one's batteries have been recharged. After sleeping for six to eight hours, one can begin the day with vigor and drive. Each and every night this miracle happens anew. One may be completely exhausted; however, almost always, after a good night's sleep, one is recharged.

After an exhausting and sometimes discouraging day, we go to sleep weary and weak, and Hashem awakens us the next morning refreshed and renewed. Every morning we must thank Hashem for this successful operation. Where does this strength come from? It is a G-d-given blessing, a miniature form of *techiyas hameisim* (revival of the dead).

In addition, we should be thankful that although we may have tired spells throughout the day, we may suddenly feel a surge of energy that assists us to accomplish our goals.

Sometimes we may feel depressed and down, but all we really need is a breath of Hashem's fresh air. This is just another way Hashem provides strength to the weary. Try this if you are ever feeling overwhelmed — go outside and breathe deeply, or at least open a window and fill your lungs. When your body is invigorated by the influx of Hashem's cool, moist and moving air you may feel better.

"Air is the most delectable of all drinks and it provides almost immediate benefits. Drink deeply of G-d's bountiful champagne and thank Him for it" (Rabbi Avigdor Miller, *Sing, You Righteous*, pg. 315).

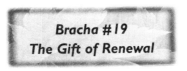

Bracha #19
The Gift of Renewal

בָּרוּךְ אַתָּה ה' אֱלֹקֵינוּ מֶלֶךְ הָעוֹלָם,
הַמַּעֲבִיר שֵׁנָה מֵעֵינָי וּתְנוּמָה מֵעַפְעַפָּי.

"Blessed are You, Eternal Master, our G-d, King of the universe,
Who removes sleep from my eyes and slumber from my eyelids."

❧ ❧ ❧

In this bracha we thank Hashem for removing sleep from our eyes. Sometimes, after eight hours of sleep, we awake and still don't feel totally refreshed. Hashem's gift of water helps to remove the lingering sleep from our eyes. Once we wash our face we are stimulated to be grateful to Hashem for our becoming refreshed and wide awake. The Creator endows us with this renewed enthusiasm, a potential spiritual energy that can be used in the service of Hashem. This is another great *chesed* from Hashem.

Included in the gift of sleep is the wondrous process called "forgetting." Sometimes one may suffer a misfortune which makes one feel terrible. Eventually one may fall asleep and awaken in the morning a new person. One's mind is healed with the process of forgetting. "If not for forgetting, one would never be relieved of sorrow… and nothing would afford one pleasure when one remembers the misfortunes of the world…" (*Chovos Halevovos, bechina* 5).

The Talmud connects the blessing "who removes sleep from my eyes" to the washing of one's face in the morning because this process helps us feel like new. We can also remind ourselves about the versatility of water, which we not only use for drinking and cleaning, but which has the ability to refresh as well. We must be thankful for both the feeling of rejuvenation and for the miracle of water that refreshes.

We then continue with a prayer that we should merit to continually engage in Hashem's Torah and cling to His mitzvos… "may Hashem bestow on us His benevolent kindness. Thank you Hashem… Who bestows good kindness upon His people Israel." (This concluding blessing encompasses all of the blessings mentioned above.)

As stated openly in *Devarim* (10:13) we know that Hashem loves Yisroel more than the entire universe, for it says, "Behold, to Hashem are the Heavens, the earth and all therein, but He delights and loves solely your ancestors and you…" This idea is further reinforced in other places in Tanach. "'I love you,' says Hashem"… (*Malachi* 1:2). "You are Hashem's children" (*Devarim* 14:1).

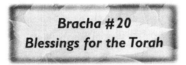

Bracha #20
Blessings for the Torah

בָּרוּךְ אַתָּה ה' אֱלֹקֵינוּ מֶלֶךְ הָעוֹלָם, אֲשֶׁר קִדְּשָׁנוּ
בְּמִצְוֹתָיו, וְצִוָּנוּ לַעֲסוֹק בְּדִבְרֵי תוֹרָה:

"Blessed are You, Eternal Master, our G-d, King of the universe,
Who has sanctified us with His commandments and
commanded us to toil in Torah study."

In these three blessings for the Torah, we thank Hashem for
allowing us to involve ourselves in Torah learning. To work
in learning, to strive to understand Torah, is a tremendous
pleasure, in addition to being the greatest *mitzvah* we have:
"*Talmud Torah* is equal to all other mitzvos" (*Shabbos* 127a).

Ben Ish Chai, in his *Sefer Halachos* on Chumash, com-
menting on people who cannot learn all day, suggests that if
one must work eight hours a day, he still has eight hours to
learn. With twenty-four hours in a day, eight hours should
be designated to learn (which includes learning with one's
children) eight hours for work and eight hours to sleep.
Women also say these blessings (*Shulchan Aruch* 47:14)

because although they are absolved from the heavier Talmud study, women have plenty of Torah to learn regarding all of the laws that apply to them (*Biur Halacha*, ibid).

> **There are 304,805 letters in the Torah. Most Sifrei Torah require 62 pieces of parchment.**

It is a tremendous blessing that Hashem has given us such a vast Torah to keep us busy, for it is a study that we must regularly engage all of our efforts into in order to be successful.

Bracha #21
Blessings for the Torah

וְהַעֲרֶב־נָא ה' אֱלֹקֵינוּ אֶת־דִּבְרֵי תוֹרָתְךָ בְּפִינוּ...

"Please sweeten, Eternal Master, our G-d, the words of Your Torah in our mouths…"

ക ക ക

In this blessing, we ask Hashem to help us enjoy the *geshmack* (pleasure) of Torah, which is the greatest *geshmack* there is. When we partake and indulge in the Torah's sweetness, we will develop to become "those who know Your Name and who learn Torah for its own sake."

Torah study is the only mitzvah and the sole pleasure for which the preliminary bracha is a Torah requirement (*mid'Oraysa*). We must be most grateful to Hashem for this greatest of all benefits. Perhaps the three brachos for Torah study correspond to all three types of brachos which the Ramabam teaches (see pages 4-5).

Bracha #22
Blessings for the Torah

בָּרוּךְ אַתָּה ה' אֱלֹקֵינוּ מֶלֶךְ הָעוֹלָם, אֲשֶׁר בָּחַר בָּנוּ מִכָּל הָעַמִּים...

"Blessed are You, Eternal Master, our G-d, King of the universe,
Who has chosen us from among all the nations."

ᘒ ᘒ ᘒ

The Torah is an exclusive gift to us. Hashem gave us His Torah because He said, "with a great and eternal love I love them" (the bracha before *Shema*).

For the gift of His Torah alone we are obligated to sing and dance all day long. On Simchas Torah we attempt to do just that, but we should remember and appreciate the Torah every day of the year, because Hashem has given us such an incredible gift.

We include in our thanks to Hashem three major ele-

> The pieces of parchment in a Torah scroll are sewn together with *gidon*—sinews and tendons of kosher animals.

ments concerning Torah study:

1. The toil and labor in learning Torah, without which it is impossible to know Torah (*Megillah* 6b).

2. The delight and pleasure of Torah study—"Please make the words of Your Torah pleasant in our mouths."

3. We refer to the intense love and happiness of our good fortune to be linked with genuine Torah study, as mentioned repeatedly in *Tehillim* 119:

☞ "In the way of Your testimonies I have rejoiced as much as in all riches" (verse 14).

☞ "In Your laws, I delight myself, I will not forget Your words" (verse 16).

☞ "My soul breaks in yearning for Your judgments at all times" (verse 20).

☞ "Also Your testimonies are my delight, my counselors" (verse 24).

☞ "And I take delight in Your commandments, which I love" (verse 47).

☞ "Your statutes were to me as songs" (verse 54).

☞ "The law of Your mouth is better for me than thousands of gold and silver" (verse 72).

☞ "Oh, how I loved Your Torah! All day long it is my

conversation" (verse 97).

ᴥ "How sweet are Your words to my palate, more than honey to my mouth" (verse 103).

ᴥ "Your testimonies are my eternal heritage,because they are the joy of my heart" (verse 111).

ᴥ "I open my mouth wide with enthusiasm because I yearn for Your commandments" (verse 131).

As we recite the blessings before we study Torah, we pray that we merit experiencing the sweetness of G-d's Torah. Our devotion to the pursuit of Torah knowledge should develop into the most intense pleasure, happiness and excitement of our lives. Daily we should remember — "the Torah that Moshe commanded us is an inheritance to the Jewish community" (*Devarim* 33:4).

Bracha # 23
Mitzvah of Tzitzis

בָּרוּךְ אַתָּה ה' אֱלֹקֵינוּ מֶלֶךְ הָעוֹלָם,
אֲשֶׁר קִדְּשָׁנוּ בְּמִצְוֹתָיו, וְצִוָּנוּ עַל מִצְוַת צִיצָת.

"Blessed are You, Eternal Master, our G-d, King of the universe, Who made us holy with His commandments, and commanded us concerning the mitzvah of tzitzis."

ᴥ ᴥ ᴥ

"And you will look upon it and remember all the commandments of Hashem" (*Bamidbar* 15:37). The mitzvah of tzitzis is a reminder of all the other mitzvos. We have to thank Hashem for this unique reminder-mitzvah. It serves as a uniform Jewish males wear to remind them of who they are. The *Gemara Shabbos* (32b) states: When Moshiach comes, those who wear tzitzis properly will merit 2,800 servants. Why 2,800? There are fringes on four corners of the tzitzis, and there are seventy nations. Ten gentiles from each nation will grab hold of each corner and beg, "May I serve you? For you know Hashem!" (*Zechariah* 8:23). Four corners x 70 nations x 10 from each nation = 2,800.

Why is this the measure for measure reward for the mitzvah of tzitzis? *Tzitzis* remind us that we are Hashem's *servants*. Hashem says: "For being My servant and accepting My mitzvos, I will reward you with a staff commensurate to the commandment of tzitzis, which is the reminder for all the other mitzvos." Thus, Hashem will give all of His servants 2,800 servants to assist them in their service to Him. 2,800 servants will be nice but we have to plan what we are going to do with them. We have to have great goals for Hashem's service that will make use of thousands of assistants.

Why does the mitzvah of tzitzis apply to garments which cover the body? This teaches us that the first step, the prerequisite to perfoming all of the mitzvos is to realize that the primary "you" is not your body, but rather your neshama, so cover the body and remember the Mitzvos!

What about females who aren't obligated to wear tzitzis? Are they losing out on this mitzvah and bracha? How will females fulfill their 100 brachos? There are various answers.

1. Females have their laws of *tznius* of dress, which is their way of wearing a badge of glory that demonstrates that they are members of Hashem's holy people.

2. Females do have the mitzvah of viewing the tzitzis that their husbands and sons wear. When the Torah says: "and you will see it" (*Bamidbar* 15:39), the Talmud says: "It is seen by others" (*Shabbos* 27b).

When girls and women happen to notice tzitzis, they will think, "Ah, that reminds me of our role as Hashem's people, I should keep in mind to make sure to fulfill the mitzvos."

3. Some hold that females do not have the obligation of saying all 100 brachos daily. Others say there are enough extra brachos that they can still make the count of 100. When we study the context of the source of the obligation of 100 brachos in the Talmud (*Menachos* 43b) we find a sequence of three teachings:

I. One who wears tefillin and tzitzis is not likely to sin.

II. Wearing the royal blue *techeiles* on the tzitzis will

remind one of Hashem's throne of glory.

III. One is obligated to recite 100 blessings daily in order to express our love and fear of Hashem.

These three teachings may apply only to males who need them for the reasons previously stated. Females, however, were created by Hashem with different roles. Additionally, Hashem granted females special *binah* (understanding) (*Sotah* 35b), enabling them to reach levels of spirituality that males can reach only through performing time-generated mitzvos.

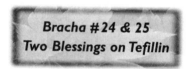

Bracha #24 & 25
Two Blessings on Tefillin

בָּרוּךְ אַתָּה ה׳ אֱלֹקֵינוּ מֶלֶךְ הָעוֹלָם,
אֲשֶׁר קִדְּשָׁנוּ בְּמִצְוֹתָיו וְצִוָּנוּ לְהָנִיחַ תְּפִלִּין.

"Blessed are You, Eternal Master, our G-d, King of the universe, Who made us holy with His commandments and commanded us to put on tefillin."

בָּרוּךְ אַתָּה ה׳ אֱלֹקֵינוּ מֶלֶךְ הָעוֹלָם,
אֲשֶׁר קִדְּשָׁנוּ בְּמִצְוֹתָיו, וְצִוָּנוּ עַל מִצְוַת תְּפִלִּין.

"Blessed are You, Eternal Master, our G-d, King of the universe, Who made us holy with His commandments and commanded us concerning the mitzvah of tefillin."

ها ها ها

There are two blessings, one for the hand and one for the head. Each tefillin contains the mention of Hashem's name twenty-one times (*Rambam, Laws of Tefillin*, ch. 4-14). Tefillin contain the teaching: "Listen Yisroel, Hashem is our G-d, Hashem is One." We learn: a male who wears tefillin, will live longer because it connects him to Hashem's name. "Hashem *aleyhem yichyu*" — "Hashem is on him, he shall live" (*Yeshaya* 38). The verse in the tefillin *shel yad,* which is worn on the arm opposite the heart, says "serve Hashem with your entire heart" (*Devarim* 6:5) to teach that we should accept Hashem into our hearts. The tefillin *shel rosh,* on the head, corresponds to the brain and urges us to concentrate on Hashem.

The tefillin are a crown Jewish males wear, a badge of aristocracy. As one of my students once said: The best part of waking up is wearing tefillin on your "*kup*".

Intermediate Prayers

בָּרוּךְ שֶׁאָמַר וְהָיָה הָעוֹלָם, בָּרוּךְ הוּא...

"Blessed be He Who spoke,
and the world came to be. Blessesd be He…"

In Baruch Sheamar we praise Hashem as
"The King Who is praised and glorified forev-

72

er." We also thank Hashem here for allowing us to praise Him.

But what is meant by the phrase, The Holy One, Blessed be He, the King Who is "praised with praises?" Don't we praise everyone with praises? Isn't this redundant? Why are we thanking Hashem for being praiseworthy? Rabbi Avigdor Miller (*Praise My Soul* p. 390) says that the more we understand Hashem's greatness, the greater we are, for, of all peoples, we are the closest to Hashem, as it says, "the Children of Israel, My intimate people" (*Tehillim 148*). Hashem is saying: "You are My chosen treasure, My closest relatives."

The *Gemara* (*Shevuos* 30b) says, "The servant to a king is like the king." Therefore, the greater the king, the greater the servant. Hence, "the King Who is praised with praises" is actually a blessing to express our gratitude for Hashem's greatness which increases our value in the world.

The *Siddur HaGra* explains that actually only Hashem can be praised with total praise because *He is perfect*. For example, when a person is praised for his diligence in learning *twenty* hours a day, the praise is limited because a person is human and cannot possibly learn for *twenty-four* hours. Hashem is the only one who never sleeps and has no mortal limitations and therefore can be truly praised with total perfection.

Our Sages tell us that the text of this blessing was composed by the Sages of the Great Assembly by means of a note that descended from heaven containing the eightyseven words of *Baruch Sheamar* (*Taz*). This explains why we should recite this blessing using a sweet tune—it is a precious, glorious, heavenly song. Every word should be studied and appreciated in depth (*Tur, Orach Chaim* ch. 51).

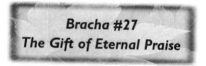

Bracha #27
The Gift of Eternal Praise

יִשְׁתַּבַּח שִׁמְךָ לָעַד מַלְכֵּנוּ...
"Praised be Your name forever, our King..."

🙦 🙦 🙦

Hashem rewards us by allowing us to praise Him. At the conclusion of *Pesukei D'zimra,* we regret that we are unable to continue saying this part of the prayers because we have to go on to the next section. Thus, we conclude that by right we should continue since "Your praises are unlimited...".

"Hashem made everything so that we would recognize Him" (*Koheles* 3:14). In this blessing we mention twice that Hashem is the King, since this is the reason we should be praising Him forever. He is the king, in control of everything, and one of the primary ways we serve Him is by always praising Him.

Bracha #28
The Gift of Light

...אוֹר חָדָשׁ עַל צִיּוֹן תָּאִיר וְנִזְכֶּה כֻלָּנוּ מְהֵרָה לְאוֹרוֹ: בָּרוּךְ אַתָּה ה' יוֹצֵר הַמְּאוֹרוֹת:

"May You cause a new light to shine upon Zion, and may we all merit quickly its light. Blessed are You, O Eternal Master, Who forms the luminaries."

ঌ ঌ ঌ

Here we thank Hashem for creating the sun and the moon. There are a multitude of ways we benefit from the luminaries. Hashem's sun provides the world with unlimited kindness. Without the sun nothing would grow. It not only produces and energizes the food we eat through photosynthesis, but it also warms up and illuminates the world, thus sustaining and maintaining all life.

125 trillion horsepower of solar energy reaches the earth each second.

At night, Hashem presents us with a glorious, luminous

moon, which we sanctify once a month. We owe special thanks to The Creator for the moon. The light at night also provides glorious pleasure when we walk down dark roads and have this magical light helping us to see.

This blessing includes the phrase: "He makes peace and creates everything." Everything in the universe works in harmony together because the one Creator is the Master Who created and controls the entire universe. But why is this linked to "He forms the light"? There are many reasons for this:

1. Only after Hashem created light did the Torah state: "It was good" for the first time (*Bereishis* 1:4). Light enables us to see all else.

2. The sun's rays provide life to all on earth. Solar energy is the battery that charges all of the processes of life.

3. The main purpose of all of creation is for people to witness Hashem's creations and recognize Him. "Hashem made everything so that all should fear/see Him." (*Koheles* 3:14).

This blessing is the longest of all of the 100 blessings we say daily. It is not only a blessing for the luminaries; it is actually a blessing for everything in the universe.

We thank Hashem for the many gifts the sun provides us, including:

ๆ   The sun's life-saving warmth;

ๆ   The light the sun provides enabling us to see and enjoy the world around us;

ๆ   The sun's life-giving vitamin D;

ๆ   The process of photosynthesis which allows all vegetation and food to exist;

ๆ   The way the sun demarcates each of our days and each season;

ๆ   The way the sun raises by evaporation from the oceans' great volumes of water which the winds blow inland to supply the world with rain…

ๆ   The light of the moon which the sun supplies.

We learn from the angels how to thank Hashem, as it says in the blessing, "For the luminaries… the angels extol You forever."

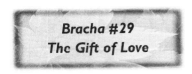

Bracha #29
The Gift of Love

אַהֲבָה רַבָּה אֲהַבְתָּנוּ...

"With a great love You have loved us…"

Hashem embraces the nation of Israel with love. The

Abishter says, "I love you" (*Malachi* 1). Hashem loves us more than the entire universe, as has been mentioned repeatedly in the Torah (see below). Hashem loves us more than we love our best friend, more than parents love their children. Hashem is the source of all love and He focuses it all on us. He loves every single Jew more than the entire universe. This leads us to appreciate the gift of His Torah, which teaches us about Hashem in the most effective way possible. From the Torah we learn about how He thinks and how He wants us to live every aspect of our lives.

> **Hashem promises**
> **"I will never forget you."**
> **(*Yeshaya*, 49:15)**

We conclude this blessing with: "Blessed are You, Hashem, Who chooses His people Yisroel with love." In a multitude of places, the Torah clearly reiterates that Hashem chose the Jewish people as His treasured nation.

✺ **Hashem chose us.** "Hashem chose you over all of the other nations. Although you are a minority, He loves you most" (*Devarim* 7:6-7).

✺ **As His children.** "Because you are His children He took you out of Egypt to serve Him and He punished those who had afflicted you (*Shemos* 4:22-23).

✺ **As His holy people.** "You shall be to Me a kingdom of ministers and a holy nation" (*Shemos* 19: 6).

🙠 **His beloved people.** "Because Hashem loves you…
He redeemed you from the house of slavery…" (*Devarim* 7:8).

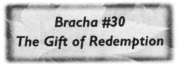

Bracha #30
The Gift of Redemption

...בָּרוּךְ אַתָּה ה' גָּאַל יִשְׂרָאֵל:

"Blessed are You, Eternal Master, Who redeemed Yisroel."

🙠 🙠 🙠

Here we bless and thank Hashem for rescuing our ances-
tors from Egypt. This is a fundamental example of how
Hashem saves us when necessary. Two hundred and fifty
miracles were performed for us when Hashem drowned the
Egyptians in the sea. This demonstrates the extent to which
Hashem will go on our behalf. (See Pesach Haggadah).

Bracha #31
The Gift of Night Time

בָּרוּךְ אַתָּה ה' אֱלֹקֵינוּ מֶלֶךְ הָעוֹלָם, אֲשֶׁר בִּדְבָרוֹ מַעֲרִיב עֲרָבִים...

"Blessed are You, Eternal Master, our G-d,
King of the Universe, Who by His word brings on evenings…"

🙠 🙠 🙠

In our evening prayers, we thank Hashem for darkness which Hashem furnishes as a respite, a treat for our benefit.

"The world was built for kindliness" (*Tehillim* 89:7), includes every feature in the universe Hashem has created — even darkness which allows us to rest. Darkness also allows the soil to rest and regain its resources. People, too, are forced to desist from their toil and they regain their strength. These are situations that Hashem has planned for our benefit.

We also speak about the stars Hashem has organized in heaven. Our sun is only one star among about a trillion others, just in our galaxy. The incredible vastness of space serves to stimulate our minds to appreciate Him, as it says: "Raise up your eyes on high to see Who created these" (*Yeshaya* 40:26). When we bless the new moon each month during the first half of the month, we say it is a form of "greeting our Father in heaven," because this serves to help us recognize the Creator.

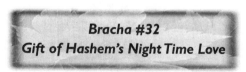

Bracha #32
Gift of Hashem's Night Time Love

אַהֲבַת עוֹלָם בֵּית יִשְׂרָאֵל עַמְּךָ אָהַבְתָּ...

"An eternal love have You loved the House of Israel, Your people."

🦎 🦎 🦎

We say this blessing before the morning Shema, as well as during the evening prayers, to acknowledge that Hashem loves us at night as well as in the morning. Night reminds us of exile, as it says, "this world is compared to night" (*Bava Metzia* 83b). This helps us remember that even though everything may look hopeless and dark, from behind the scenes Hashem still loves us. In fact, we can be sure that Hashem is always watching us and taking care of us—even if we can't see Him or His actions.

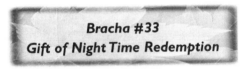

Bracha #33
Gift of Night Time Redemption

...בָּרוּךְ אַתָּה ה׳ גָּאַל יִשְׂרָאֵל:

"Blessed are You, Eternal Master, Who redeemed Yisroel."

Redemption is mentioned in the evening after the Shema as well as during the day to acknowledge that Hashem saves us even during times of distress. He is always rescuing us.

At times we may think that Hashem is the Creator Who gave and provides us with food and all other necessities, but there may be limits to what He can do for us. When we are surrounded with enemies and there seems to be no avenue of escape, what will happen to us? We therefore review the highlights of our exodus from Egypt twice a day, to remind ourselves that Hashem is in complete control, always. Whatever trouble we may be in daily, we have one—and only one—address to which we may turn.

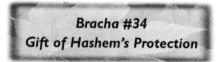

Bracha #34
Gift of Hashem's Protection

...וּשְׁמֹר צֵאתֵנוּ וּבוֹאֵנוּ, לְחַיִּים וּלְשָׁלוֹם, מֵעַתָּה
וְעַד עוֹלָם. בָּרוּךְ אַתָּה ה׳ שׁוֹמֵר עַמּוֹ יִשְׂרָאֵל לָעַד:

"Safeguard our coming and going, for life and for peace,
from now to eternity. Blessed are You, Eternal Master,
Who protects His people Yisroel forever."

&? &? &?

The *Abishter* helps us fall asleep and watches over us and takes care of us all through the night. The word "shomer," a "guard," comes from the root "shom," which means "there." A guard has to be there, on duty, to fulfill his responsibility. Hashem is the only guard Who can be all over at once. We say in *Tehillim* (23)—"Even though I am in a valley of trouble, I am not afraid, for You are with me."

Bracha #35
Gift of Hashem's Rule

בָּרוּךְ אַתָּה ה' הַמֶּלֶךְ בִּכְבוֹדוֹ, תָּמִיד יִמְלוֹךְ...
עָלֵינוּ לְעוֹלָם וָעֶד, וְעַל כָּל מַעֲשָׂיו:

"Blessed are You, Eternal Master, the King in His glory, Who will always rule over us, forever and for all eternity, and over all His creations."

The *Abishter*, in His honor and glory and in all that He does throughout the universe, is still primarily our King. He does everything with us in mind.

We say in Hodu, "He is Hashem our G-d; His judgements are all over the world." This means that Hashem considers us the main actors, so to speak, on the scene of history. All else is background scenery. Since He is our king, He dictates how we should act and we obey His commands.

In the Shabbos Morning prayer, we say ישמחו במלכתך — "They will rejoice in Your rulership." Hashem is the source of all mercy, goodness and kindness. His control is always with kindness. Thus, the more He manifests His rulership over us, the more we benefit and rejoice.

Shemoneh Esrei

*I*n this silent, standing prayer we arrive at the climax of our prayers. All of our previous prayers were a preparation for an audience with the King and Creator of the universe. Now we have a chance to speak directly to Hashem with these eighteen (or now nineteen) blessings which are the complete process of prayer.

The Shemoneh Esrei commences with three blessings of praise. Twelve blessings (now thirteen) of requests are then recited for all of our

Shemoneh Esrei Chart

ɞ ɞ ɞ

Bracha #1 .... Zechus Avos
Bracha #2 .... Techiyas Hameisim
Bracha #3 .... Hashem's Holiness & Perfection
Bracha #4 .... Wisdom
Bracha #5 .... Teshuva
Bracha #6 .... Forgiveness
Bracha #7 .... Daily Help
Bracha #8 .... Healing
Bracha #9 .... Abundance
Bracha #10 .... Redemption
Bracha #11 .... Justice
Bracha #12 .... Destroying the Enemy
Bracha #13 .... Support
Bracha #14 .... Jerusalem
Bracha #15 .... Salvation
Bracha #16 .... Hashem's Attention
Bracha #17 .... Hashem's Favor
Bracha #18 .... Thanks
Bracha #19 .... Peace

needs. Finally, three more blessings are recited as we take leave of Hashem.

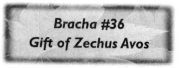

Bracha #36
Gift of Zechus Avos

‎...בָּרוּךְ אַתָּה ה׳ מָגֵן אַבְרָהָם:

"Blessed are You, Eternal Master, shield of Avraham."

❧ ❧ ❧

In the first blessing of Shemoneh Esrei, we refer to Avraham. Hashem defends us and pro-

Bracha #1 of Shemoneh Esrei

tects us. He is our shield. He always takes care of us because we are the descendants of Avraham, our ancestor, who was called Hashem's best friend.

This first blessing of this group (the bracha called *Avos*) is the most important of the entire Shemoneh Esrei. In fact, if one fails to concentrate during this blessing, it is as if one has failed to pray at all (*Shulchan Aruch, Orach Chayim*, 101). Thus, it is essential to do one's best to learn to understand, appreciate, and keep in mind the process of prayer, which is "actually standing before the King," and to relate to the words in a realistic way as one who is privileged to address the King.

The Mesilas Yeshorim (ch. 19) describes this concept:

"We must analyze this matter and contemplate it properly...we are actually standing in front of the Creator, May His Name be blessed, and we are encouraged to discuss our needs with Hashem, although we are unable to see Him...We must fix the truth of this matter in our heart/mind...We are actually addressing Hashem, pleading and entreating Him! Hashem, *Yisborach Shemo*, is listening attentively to us as one who listens to a friend..."

Before beginning the silent prayer of Shemoneh Esrei we take a moment to focus our mind, and, as we say the first six words, we should concentrate on the meaning of each of these words:

Blessed—You are the source of all blessing. We bow down to You now in humility and gratitude.

Are You—We address You directly.

Hashem—The *Shulchan Aruch* (ch. 5) defines Hashem's Name as referring to:

ے His mastery over everything, which includes the understanding that Hashem created the universe and that He has complete control over every aspect of its existence.

ے His eternal existence—He was *always*, He is *always*, and He will *always* exist.

Our G-d — This refers to Hashem's unlimited power and His complete control over all matter and energy. The possessive suffix ("nu," which means "our") indicates that Hashem has chosen us as His people and that He serves as our Father and King to guide and protect us with special devotion.

"And the G-d of our Fathers—G-d of Avraham, G-d of Yitzchak, and G-d of Yaakov"

This phrase contains no mention of *malchus*, which is usually required in every bracha. However, mentioning Avraham substitutes for the required mention of *malchus* in every bracha, because Avraham Avinu taught the whole world that Hashem is the King of the universe (*Tosfos, Brachos* 40b).

Avraham, Yitzchak and Yaakov, and Sarah, Rivkah, Rachel and Leah were uniquely considered the fathers and mothers of the Jewish nation (*Brachos* 16b) because of the perfection they achieved and transmitted to their children for all generations.

Avraham, according to Rambam (*Avodas Kochavim* 1:2) is called the pillar of the world since he was the first to denounce idol worship and recognize Hashem as the Almighty, Eternal Creator and Controller of the universe.

He then founded the Torah nation through teaching and raising a family that would devote their lives to serve Hashem.

Yitzchak offered his life for the service of Hashem and lived a life of service to Hashem in Eretz Yisroel.

Yaakov went into exile where he produced and established the twelve *shevotim* — the core of the nation that would go on to receive the Torah and devote their lives to serving Hashem.

"the G-d"

This refers to Hashem's power which He uses completely for the sake of bestowing kindness (*Tosfos, Rosh Hashanah* 17b), beginning with the creation of the universe and continuing with the ongoing support and maintenance of all life.

"Who is great, mighty, and awesome"

This phrase is from *Devarim* (10:17) where Rabbeinu Bechayei says it refers to Hashem's great kindliness, His mighty justice, and His awe-inspiring mercy.

The Rosh differs with Tosfos and considers this phrase to be the mention of *malchus* in this bracha. Perhaps both opinions complement each other because Avraham Avinu taught Hashem's *malchus*, and this phrase, "Who is great, mighty, and awesome" is the substance of what Avraham taught by his emulating Hashem's ways and by his teachings.

"G-d, Most High"

Hashem is above everything, the Cause of all existence and the Activator of all that transpires.

"Who bestows good kindnesses"

Is not all kindness good? Only Hashem's kindnesses are perfectly good, without any side-effects. In addition, His kindnesses are everlasting (*Tehillim* 136).

"And He possesses everything"

Thus, 1. Hashem is not indebted to anyone, so that His kindnesses are pure — without any ulterior motives — and

2. He has everything at His disposal to provide the most kindness to everyone at all times with His unlimited resources.

"And He remembers the kindnesses of the Fathers"

This phrase explains that Hashem chose our forefathers because of their acts of *chesed*. This phrase is linked to the previous phrase — because they did *chesed*, they received *chasodim* from Hashem (measure for measure). This also

> **All the kindness Hashem bestows on us always is due to our forefathers (Rambam).**

reminds us that the more we emulate our forefathers, the worthier we become to merit Hashem's favor!

"And He brings a Redeemer to their descendants"

Hashem is continuously providing and preparing the best kindness for His beloved ones.

"For the sake of His Name, with love"

Hashem's Name describes His essence [Eternal Master], which also includes His eternal kindness of giving us an Afterlife. Thus, the ultimate redemption—with Moshiach's arrival—will be the climax of the gift that Hashem will bestow on our forefathers' descendants.

"The King Who helps, saves, and shields"

Hashem has countless ways of saving us and many agents to perform His constant rescue work.

"Blessed are You, Shield of Avraham"

This concluding blessing is the climax and summary of this bracha. Hashem's Name is intertwined (so to speak) with that of Avraham Avinu. It was Avraham who taught us about Hashem and Hashem loves us because Avraham loved Hashem (*Yeshaya* 41:8).

Hashem is willing to shield us when we follow in Avraham Avinu's footsteps! (Actually, this is an understatement. The truth is that Hashem is already our shield, but the more we recognize this truth, the more we will reap the benefits.)

This blessing is the most important one of the Shemoneh Esrei because it teaches the basics of prayer and our relationship with Hashem. We stress the *zechusim* of the Avos (the merits of our ancestors) and Hashem's kindness to them and to us. This is how we get in the door for an appointment with Hashem. This is the reason He listens to us.

Bracha #37
Gift of Techiyas Hameisim

...בָּרוּךְ אַתָּה ה' מְחַיֵּה הַמֵּתִים:

"...Blessed are You, Eternal Master, Who revives the dead."

෯ ෯ ෯

Hashem's power is unequalled in each and every dimension. This bracha gives examples of Hashem's might, but it begins and concludes with the fact that Hashem revives

**Bracha #2 of
Shemoneh Esrei**

the dead, since *techiyas hameisim* is the ultimate demonstration of Hashem's power. Not only does Hashem give life, He also recreates life by reviving the righteous dead who deserve eternal reward.

Two Key Lessons

Rabbi Yochanon offers two teachings which help explain this bracha:

1. "Three keys are exclusively in the Almighty's possession: the keys of childbirth, rain and the revival of the dead" (*Taanis* 2a).

2. "Wherever you find Hashem's might, you will also find His humility [kindness]" (*Taanis* 29).

Hashem's greatness and power are always directed towards helping and bestowing kindness. This blessing intertwines Hashem's might with what He uses it for—providing life in different forms and stages.

Sleep

Included in the praise "Who revives the dead" is the fact that Hashem daily wakes people from their sleep. According to the Talmud (*Brachos* 57b), sleep is considered a form of death [a sixtieth part]. The process of sleep, which refreshes and rejuvenates the body, is a stupendous miracle through which Hashem's power can be recognized and appreciated.

When we say, "You uphold the fallen, heal the sick, and set loose the bound," we are itemizing some of the details included in the gift of life that Hashem gives to the dead. The gift of life consists of mobility, health, and millions of additional miracles performed by Hashem (Rabbi Avigdor Miller, *Praise, My Soul*, pg. 383).

Concept of Death

In this bracha, we note the great Torah teaching that death is merely a form of sleep in the program of eternal life. Death is one of Hashem's kindnesses to prepare people for the afterlife and the revival of the dead.

People are given life on this earth to fulfill the Torah and mitzvos. Our goal is to generate *zechusim* (merits), which are the preparation required to gain entry to Olam Habah. Death is a transition and a "sleeping" time similar to sleep at night.

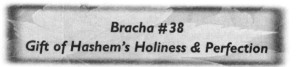

Bracha #38
Gift of Hashem's Holiness & Perfection

בָּרוּךְ אַתָּה ה' הָקֵל הַקָּדוֹשׁ...

"...Blessed are You, Eternal Master, the Al-mighty, the Holy One."

🖝 🖝 🖝

The more we understand Hashem's greatness, the more we recognize our own potential greatness, because we are Hashem's closest people. This bracha is the third of the group of blessings that praise Hashem. To summarize:

Bracha #3 of Shemoneh Esrei

1. *Avos* – Our great Fathers opened our eyes to the praises of Hashem.

2. *Gevuros* – Hashem's mighty deeds demonstrate His greatness.

3. *Kedusha* – Both of these sources add up to teaching Hashem's unequalled, supreme perfection!

A Unique Message

When we say that Hashem is holy, wise, and perfect we should not think that these words are used in an ordinary sense. His holiness is so extraordinary that the "holy ones [angels and the holy Jewish nation] praise You daily forever." As we say in *Tehillim* (145:3), "There is no end to understanding His greatness."

Role Models

There are two lessons we are required to learn from the angels who praise Hashem:

1. To praise Him [*hallel*] with enthusiasm.

2. To do it regularly, on a daily basis, as much as we can.

Three Reasons We Thank Hashem For His Holiness

We conclude this blessing with an expression of thanks to Hashem for being Holy. "Blessed are You Hashem, the Holy G-d." What is the significance of this thanks?

Rabbi Avigdor Miller gives three explanations:

1. Hashem's superiority elevates our greatness since He chose us as His people.

2. Our eternal reward—which is based on being in His presence, is linked to Hashem's greatness.

3. Through studying His unique greatness and attaching ourselves to His ways we improve and gain perfection.

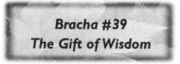

Bracha #39
The Gift of Wisdom

בָּרוּךְ אַתָּה ה' חוֹנֵן הַדָּעַת...

"…Blessed are You, Hashem, gracious Giver of wisdom."

 ه{ ههذ ههذ

We now begin six blessings where we offer praise and thanks, and then voice our requests for our individual needs.

In the first blessing, we thank Hashem for giving us the

ability to think.

This is our first petition to Hashem in Shemoneh Esrei.

Bracha #4 of Shemoneh Esrei

The ability to think is the first and foremost of our needs from Hashem. We beg for intellect, without which we would differ little from animals. Without the ability to think and accumulate knowledge, all else would be lacking. The first step in getting anywhere is to be able to think. Afterwards, we ask for health, wealth, redemption, etc.

The Source

In only this prayer/request we preface with a statement of fact: Before we ask for our needs, we praise Hashem, the One and only source of knowledge and understanding. Why is this emphasized?

When the Torah (*Devarim* 8:18) cautions us not to forget that Hashem is the One Who provides us with the power to accomplish, the *Targum* interprets: "For He is the One Who provides you with the *insights* to acquire possessions."

All our achievements begin with our minds—which cannot function or even exist without Hashem!

From simple thinking to the heights of complex intelligence, from abstract analysis to practical applications, from deducing complicated issues to unraveling the depths of the

Torah—Hashem's aid is essential!

A Gift

The word "*chonain*" חֹנֵן (granting of a favor) is used three times in this blessing to indicate our request of a gift. The *sedrah* in the Torah (*Devarim* 3:23) which begins with the word וָאֶתְחַנַּן, "*Voeschanan*," contains Moshe Rabbeinu's request to Hashem for the right to enter Eretz Yisroel. Underlying Moshe's request was his desire to be close to Hashem through experiencing the actual entry to, living in, and fulfilling the mitzvos pertaining to the promised land.

Thus, there is a parallel here between our daily prayers for the gift of *daas* (profound knowledge) and Moshe's plea to Hashem to enter Eretz Yisroel. Like Moshe, we too desire to learn more about Hashem and grow closer to Him.

The Rambam (*Teshuva* 9:2) takes the whole issue a step further. He explains that the primary reason Jews hope and pray for Moshiach's arrival is the wish to gain increased knowledge and wisdom, as is taught in *Yeshaya*, "The earth will then be full of wisdom..." (11:9).

Thus the quest for wisdom should be our chief desire in life and the reason for our existence. The Gemara strengthens this idea, "There is no poverty besides the lack of *daas* (knowledge), and there is no wealth besides *daas*" (*Nedarim* 41a).

Additionally, the main difference between humans and animals is that people can acquire knowledge and gain wisdom. Humans have access to developing *deah* — clarity of knowledge, *binah* — the ability to analyze and deduce one thing from another, and *sechel* — the practical applications of wisdom.

The Secret

How does one gain wisdom?

In *Mishlei* (2) it states: "Hashem provides wisdom, from His mouth [comes] knowledge and understanding."

The Gemara (*Niddah* 70b) explains that the only way to gain true wisdom is to work for it and to request it from the Master/Creator/Owner of all wisdom.

In Rashi's comment on *Niddah* 70b, he says that "wisdom is given to those who love Hashem, from His mouth, not from any other source." In order to achieve wisdom, one must love Hashem and request this gift from the Source."

Memory

Memory, like wisdom, is one facet of a keen mind. Rashi (*Avodah Zarah* 8a) teaches: "One who forgets his learning should focus more on this prayer/request."

All forms of wisdom are to be gained from concentrating on this prayer with intense desire.

Bracha #40
The Gift of Teshuva

...בָּרוּךְ אַתָּה ה' הָרוֹצֶה בִּתְשׁוּבָה.

"Blessed are You, Eternal Master, Who desires repentance."

෴ ෴ ෴

Hashem loves us and provides us with many ways to return to Him if we fall by the wayside. This request concerning repentance follows the prayer for intellect because it is our next most urgent need. As soon as our mind clears we realize that our purpose in this world is to make something of ourselves by coming closer to Hashem.

We refer to Hashem here [and in the next bracha] as our Father and as our King—signifying we must both love and fear Hashem. These two metaphors describe our basic relationship with Hashem.

The Rambam, at the beginning of his work "The Fundamentals of the Torah" says, "We have a mitzvah to love and fear Hashem, Who is most honored and revered, as it says..." (*Yesodai HaTorah*, ch. 2).

Love and fear are the two pillars of our relationship with

Hashem. Similarly, the Ramban says that all the positive commandments of the Torah are supported by the pillar of love of Hashem, while the negative prohibitions stand on the pillar of fear of Hashem.

We now focus on three levels of *teshuva*:

1. We ask Hashem to help us return to His Torah

The *Alei Shur* (1:236) explains that the most essential ingredient in a *teshuva* program is Torah knowledge.

In fact, we are continually urged to: "Make your Torah study a permanent activity"(*Pirkei Avos* 1:15), and "Reduce your business activities and engage in Torah study" (*Pirkei Avos* 4:12).

We will be assisted in our quest for perfect *teshuva* if we develop a daily, regular Torah study program, with time for in depth Torah analysis, review time, halacha study, learning *mussar*, etc. Each area of Torah study will help us improve in various areas of our life.

2. We ask Hashem to help us return to His *avodah*

In the second part of this prayer we ask Hashem to help us improve in our behavior as His servant. The Torah teaches us how to serve Hashem and relate to Him as to One who has the ultimate authority.

3. We ask Hashem to help us return to perfect repentance.

We conclude this prayer by asking for perfect repentance, which consists of twenty steps (see *Shaarei Teshuva*, ch. 1 and *Chovos Halevovos*, section on *teshuva*) which will eventually lead us completely into Hashem's presence.

When we pray for *teshuva*, we ask Hashem:

For mercy and atonement for all of our sins,

To erase our sins and re-accept us,

To assist us in repentance and help us overcome our evil inclination (*Shaarei Teshuva* 1:41).

How does one begin to do teshuva?

Ask Hashem for Help!
How does one continue doing teshuva?
Continue asking for Hashem's Help!

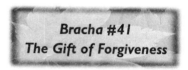

Bracha #41
The Gift of Forgiveness

בָּרוּךְ אַתָּה ה' חַנּוּן הַמַּרְבֶּה לִסְלֹחַ....

"Blessed are You, Eternal Master, Gracious One, Who generously forgives."

In this next blessing we bless Hashem for forgiving us.

This is not presumptuous for we acknowledge that Hashem forgives us continually. Even though we repeatedly commit the same sins, the *Abishter* still says: "Come back, come back and I will forgive you."

Hashem knows we are human. He created us and keeps challenging us. He wants us to keep improving. "A tzaddik falls seven times but he keeps on rising" (*Mishlei* 24:16).

We request forgiveness from:

1. *Our Father* (we love You dearly).

2. *Our King* (we respect You greatly).

In order to receive forgiveness from Hashem, our Father, we have to work on respecting and honoring our mortal parents. "When one denies gratitude to other people, it is as if one denies it to Hashem" (*Koheles Rabbah* 7:4).

How do we revere and honor our parents? When we assist them, speak highly of them, and think about them with respect.

As we improve our relations with our human parents, we will deserve their forgiveness and in return Hashem will help us improve our relationship with Him to be deserving of His forgiveness.

When we fully recognize, accept, proclaim, and relate to

Hashem as our Father and King, we will be deserving of His forgiveness.

To think of Hashem as our *King* we need to focus on the following: Hashem is in complete control of everything around us. His power, wisdom, and kindness are unequalled and unlimited. We fear Hashem as our King and as our *Father*.

Hashem created us. He loves us. He sustains us. He provided us with our bodies and souls, and He continues to provide the necessities and joys of life. He desires our prayers. He consents to assist us.

Suggestion: Each time you say this blessing, concentrate on one particular sin for which you desire forgiveness from Hashem. Some examples would be wasting time and not spending more time on Torah study, failure to concentrate more on one's purpose in life, not doing more chesed, speaking loshon hora, not respecting one's parents, etc.

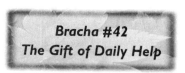

Bracha #42
The Gift of Daily Help

...בָּרוּךְ אַתָּה ה׳ גּוֹאֵל יִשְׂרָאֵל.

"Blessed are You, Eternal Master, Redeemer ("Goel") of Israel."

❧ ❧ ❧

The *Abishter* repeatedly saves us from trouble. *"Goal"* (see Bracha # 30) literally means He has saved us in the past. But *"goel"* means He always rescues us — right now and forever.

Bracha #7 of Shemoneh Esrei

The Gemara (*Megillah* 17b) asks: "Why is the subject of redemption the seventh of the 18 blessings?"

Rava explains: "Because the final redemption will be during a seventh year [*shemitta*]..."

Rashi (*ibid.*) then asks: "Why is this bracha placed here? This is *not* a prayer for the final redemption from exile. Those requests are placed later in *Brachos* 10, 14, and 15 [of Shemoneh Esrei]. Nevertheless, Rashi answers, "this bracha is related to the issue of redemption, since it deals with redemption from the *tzoros* that we regularly suffer. Therefore, it was positioned as the seventh bracha."

1. Consider someone whose home or shop window was broken by a rock-throwing delinquent; or whose car was broken into and spare tire was stolen; or whose tax return was audited by the U.S. Internal Revenue Service because their charitable deductions [20%] appeared disproportionately large.

These are just a few examples of the many needs this blessing refers to. We need help, and Hashem is our only true source of help! When we say this blessing we are asking for Hashem's help for these kinds of *tzoros*.

2. The year of *shemitta* teaches us that Hashem is the Master of the Universe. He owns our land as He owns everything else. We have been placed in this world to learn this lesson. Once we achieve this perfection, we will be deserving of the redemption.

3. Why does Hashem send *tzoros* to people? For our own benefit! *Tzoros* are meant to wake us up, to help us realize that we always need Hashem's help. When we pray to Hashem for help, we demonstrate that we are learning the lesson and, therefore, Hashem helps us.

Bracha #43
The Gift of Healing

בָּרוּךְ אַתָּה ה׳ רוֹפֵא חוֹלֵי עַמּוֹ יִשְׂרָאֵל...

"Blessed are You, Eternal Master, Who heals the sick of His people, Israel."

 crc crc crc

Behind all of the hospitals and all doctors is the *Abishter*. The *Abishter* is the only Healer we should have faith in. He has many messengers, but He is the Healer. If you go to a dentist, it is as if the *Abishter* is filling in

Bracha #8 of Shemoneh Esrei

your cavities. The *Abishter* has a staff; an entire array of legions at His command.

This prayer for healing is positioned as the eighth blessing of Shemoneh Esrei for a specific reason. The *Gemara* (*Megillah* 17b) explains the mitzvah of bris milah is performed when a male child is eight days old. The baby requires healing after this mitzvah and thus the connection of this bracha to eight.

However, we may ask the following questions:

☞ Why is the issue of bris milah relevant throughout a male's life?

☞ How is this reason potent enough to be the determining factor for connecting this bracha to number eight?

☞ Circumcision is a mitzvah which the Torah obligates us to perform. How does that typify ordinary illnesses which may occur due to a person's shortcomings?

> לעולם יבקש אדם
> רחמים שלא יחלה
> **A person should always pray for mercy not to become ill (*Shabbos* 32a).**

The answer to these questions may be that milah teaches the purpose of illness and the purpose of prayer in general.

Hashem obligates us to perform milah as an improvement and benefit to males who become sanctified, elevated, bonded, and attached by this blood covenant with Hashem. At the same time, healing is required.

> It took giving up the best manual on healing to learn the greatest lesson of health—Hashem is the true source of healing!

So, too, when a person is ill, it is a blow inflicted by Hashem, Who, as a Father, chastises His children when they slack off in their achievements. Thus, we pray for healing with this realization in mind. Hashem is calling our attention to improve our ways and return to Him.

You may now wonder about the specific reasons people may become ill in the first place. You may ask how precious would a remedy book for every imaginable illness be?

Well, you're in for a surprise!

Our Sages tell that there was such an authoritative book, but it was banned! The Jewish government, led by King Chizkiyahu and sanctioned by the Sages, outlawed and concealed this work.

Rashi explains that this was done because people were not being humbled by their illnesses since they would be cured immediately (*Pesachim* 56a).

Rashi further explains that this was done to force people *to pray to* Hashem for mercy, instead of simply relying on a book (*Brachos* 10b).

Health Insurance

Thus, we learn that illness is a Heaven-sent inspiration to *humble* a person and cause him or her to pray. An illness weakens the body, stirs the mind, awakens us from our stupor and motivates us to spiritual achievement. When one improves one's ways, one deserves to be physically healed as well.

This is also the message of bris milah.

Why are we obligated to cut off the foreskin of a male infant? We are instructed by Hashem to do so for many reasons, including that this permanently imprints on the boy's body what his purpose is in life:

> A cough can expel an object stuck in one's throat in a blast that can reach up to 200 miles per hour.

1. to serve Hashem,
2. to recognize Him, and
3. to realize that Hashem is needed to heal us and assist us in every step we take.

This prayer for healing, which we say three times a day, reminds us that we always need to call out to Hashem sincerely, with humble prayer. The more we realize we truly need Hashem, the more He will respond to help us.

When our attitude is healed, physical healing is just a call to Hashem away!

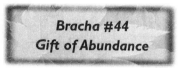

Bracha #44
Gift of Abundance

...בָּרוּךְ אַתָּה ה׳ מְבָרֵךְ הַשָּׁנִים.

"...Blessed are You, Eternal Master, Who blesses the years."

Hashem blesses us with a livelihood, sustenance and prosperity. Who is the owner of all the banks? Hashem. "Is not all silver and gold Mine?" (*Chaggai* 2:8). Hashem has a system to maintain an illusion that your livelihood comes from the bank, from your employer, from your clients/customers or from the stock market. In reality, however, it is all from the *Abishter*.

Bracha #9 of Shemoneh Esrei

Why do we suggest to Hashem here how He should bless us, even to the extent that we specify such points as our need for "dew and rain" in the winter, our desire for all the species of produce, and our longing to merit a year like the good years?

This brings us to one of the secrets of prayer, explained by the *Chovos Halevovos* (*Cheshbon Hanefesh* 3:18):

"We don't specify our needs in order to inform Hashem, since He is well aware of everything and knows exactly what is good for us and the best way to make each of us wealthy. The purpose, however, is to make *us* aware of our urgent need for His help."

By thinking about how Hashem can help us, we remind ourselves that we are completely in His hands, and we are happy knowing that Hashem knows what is best for us.

The Format

In this blessing we request:

1. **Blessings** — for the year [time frame], all the different kinds of produce [product], for the face of the earth [vehicle of production] and

2. **Satiation** — we use the term "tov" [goodness] three times: once "for goodness," once "from Your goodness," and lastly "as the good years."

We ask Hashem here to direct His benefits to us for our maximum benefit, not just to give us what we think we want, but for what He knows will satisfy us.

As the *Chovos Halevovos* concludes: "If, in my foolishness, I request that which would be detrimental, please do not fulfill my request, but do what You know is best for me!"

To Become Wealthy

One who desires wealth is urged to pray for mercy from

Hashem Who owns all wealth (*Niddah* 70b).

The Mishna Berurah (1:15) quotes the sefer *Seder Hayom:* "One should entreat Hashem to please send us our *parnosah* through a means that is: gentle, not difficult; permissible, not forbidden."

(This corresponds to the *Gemara* in *Kiddushin* 82a that one should teach one's son a profession that is clean and easy.)

People tend to work all day for *parnosah*, but how much time do they spend learning and paying attention to this key prayer/blessing?

"They called to Hashem and He answered them" (*Tehillim* 99:6).

This is our daily opportunity to request a raise from our Great Boss, the owner/master of the universe. Let us be sure to open our mouths wide for Hashem to fill them up. (See *Tehillim* 81:11).

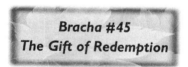

Bracha #45
The Gift of Redemption

...בָּרוּךְ אַתָּה ה׳ מְקַבֵּץ נִדְחֵי עַמּוֹ יִשְׂרָאֵל.

"...Blessed are You, Eternal Master, Who gathers in those of His nation Israel, who have been pushed away."

🙚 🙚 🙚

We have now concluded the six blessings which encompass individual needs—namely,

- intelligence,
- repentance,
- forgiveness,
- help for daily troubles,
- healing,
- wealth.

We now begin praying for the needs of the community.

Our first request is for redemption. Rashi (*Megillah* 17b) explains that blessings number 10, 14, and 15 comprise the three components of our redemption from exile: the ingathering of all Jews; the return to Yerushalayim; and the restoration of the house of Dovid.

Bracha #10 of Shemoneh Esrei

This bracha itself can be broken into three parts:

1. a prayer for freedom,
2. we should all gather together, and
3. we should become perfectly united.

A Gigantic Shofar

Why do we use a shofar to proclaim freedom?

The *Sefer Hachinuch* (331) notes that a shofar serves a dual purpose:

1. It frightens the other nations and inspires them to release their hold on us; and

2. It inspires us to accept our freedom and rise to a level of independence and subservience to the Almighty.

Together

Even now, while we live in exile, we are obligated to gather together in order to study the Torah and pray together as much as possible. The *Gemara* teaches that a *tzibbur* (group) learning or praying together has more merit than the sum of individuals that comprise it (*Avodah Zarah* 4b).

"Seek Hashem where He is to be found" (*Yeshaya* 55:6) is explained to refer to the prayers of Jews gathered as a congregation (*Yevamos* 49b).

The future ingathering of all Jews will increase our merit dramatically in an unprecedented manner. Not only will we break loose from the negative influences of the world's nations, but we will gain from the positive influences of being solely amongst each other.

Hashem will gather us together. He loves each and every Jew. He continually checks up on every Jew, and He sees to it that eventually we will all be reunited with each other and with Him.

Shemoneh Esrei

> **Bracha # 46**
> **The Gift of Justice**

בָּרוּךְ אַתָּה ה' מֶלֶךְ אוֹהֵב צְדָקָה וּמִשְׁפָּט...

"...Blessed are You, Eternal Master,
the King Who loves righteousness and justice."

❦ ❦ ❦

Bracha #11 of Shemoneh Esrei

After we pray for our independence and gathering together in unity, we realize that there will be an urgent need for leadership and guidance. Thus, we follow the request for independence and unity with a request for the return of the greatest, finest leaders the world ever saw: Moshe Rabbeinu, Aaron, Miriam, etc.

Question

As we yearn for the leaders of yesteryear, how do we understand the teaching: "One must always follow and appreciate the judges who are in his days" (*Rosh Hashanah* 25)?

There are two possible answers:

1. We are praying here that Hashem will assist our present day leaders and judges to reach the sublime heights of the ancient judges.

2. We pray for the future when we will reach new heights of greatness. When all Jews are redeemed from exile and gathered together, we will need superior judges. We are praying for all of the aspects of greatness in store for us in the near future.

An Equation

Similar to when we prayed for assistance in individual repentance and a return to Torah, the fifth bracha of Shemoneh Esrei, "*Hashivainu*," we now pray for a communal type of return: the return of the Torah's leaders—to educate, guide, judge, and bring us closer to Hashem.

Furthermore, the previously-mentioned repentance led to forgiveness (in bracha #6), redemption from troubles (#7), healing (#8), and *parnosah* (#9).

So, too, this bracha explains how we will be saved from sorrow and crying out in despair without knowing where to turn, and that we will be prepared and eager to merit Hashem's singular rule over us with kindness, mercy, and perfect judgment.

Thus, the three parts of this bracha are three separate requests which are connected:

1. The return of our leaders,
2. Relief from our troubles, and

3. A request to be solely under Hashem's Rule.

This bracha includes the prayer that Hashem should rule over us as our sole King. The conclusion of this blessing uses the word "*melech*," the only time it is used at a bracha closing in the entire Shemoneh Esrei (We do not use the word *melech* in reference to King Dovid.) The word "melech" is used here because the theme of *mishpot* (judgment) is directly related to Hashem's kingship and His complete control of the universe (*Tur* 118).

Conclusion

"King that loves righteousness and judgment." These words are found in *Bereishis* (18:19) where Hashem explains His love of Avraham Avinu because Avraham instructed his children to follow the ways of Hashem to perform righteousness and judgment.

> The more we emulate Hashem's ways of kindness and justice, the more we merit His rulership for our benefit.

The Rambam (*Deos* 1:7) explains that this means the Jewish Nation would always emulate the perfect ways of Hashem. Thus, the more we emulate Hashem's ways of kindness and justice, the more we merit His rulership for our benefit.

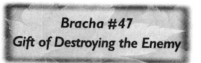

Bracha #47
Gift of Destroying the Enemy

בָּרוּךְ אַתָּה ה' שֹׁבֵר אֹיְבִים וּמַכְנִיעַ זֵדִים...

"...Blessed are You, Eternal Master,
Who breaks enemies and humbles the wicked."

ها ها ها

In this blessing, we thank Hashem Who destroys our enemies. Some are destroyed sooner, some later, but the *Abishter* is in control (*Devarim* 32:4).

Tongue Misusers

A *malshin* is someone who uses his tongue to slander and inform on others. His tongue corrupts the truth and causes destruction. Thus, a *malshin* is listed in the forefront of the evildoers who should vanish in an instant.

Bracha #12 of Shemoneh Esrei

We list four categories of enemies in this prayer: defamers, general wickedness, our enemies, and people with evil intentions.

Defining the Enemy

The *Tur* (118) points out that this prayer contains 29

words indicating that the wicked are those who deny the teachings of the Torah, which is composed of the 27 letters of the *Aleph-Bais,* and consists of two parts: the Written and Oral Law.

Most Urgent

Of all the prayers included in the Shemoneh Esrei, the prayer for punishing and destroying our enemies possesses the greatest urgency.

This is the only prayer in all of the daily davening in which we specifically ask three times for a "speedy" response (Rabbi Avigdor Miller, *Praise My Soul*, pg. 416). We beseech Hashem that the retribution be "instant," a method that is included in Hashem's system of punishment, as noted in *Bamidbar* (16:21 and 17:10).

The *Mesilas Yeshorim* (ch. 19) explains that there are three components included in the mitzvah of loving Hashem. These are: joy in serving Hashem (*simcha*), clinging to Hashem (*deveikus*), and (*kanous*) defending and upholding His Honor.

Thus, when we pray for the downfall of all the wicked, we are also engaged in the important mitzvah of loving Hashem, as it says, "Those who love Hashem hate evil!" (*Tehillim* 97:10).

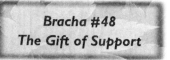

Bracha #48
The Gift of Support

...בָּרוּךְ אַתָּה ה׳ מִשְׁעָן וּמִבְטָח לַצַּדִּיקִים.

"...Blessed are You, Eternal Master,
Who supports and is the trust of the righteous."

After praying for the destruction of the wicked, we pray

**Bracha #13 of
Shemoneh Esrei**

that the righteous receive assistance. We include righteous converts as one of six groups of deserving people, since we know Hashem includes converts with the

righteous:

"Hashem loves the Righteous. Hashem guards converts" (*Tehillim* 146:8). (Also see *Vayikra* 19:32-33)

This prayer includes all of the letters of the *aleph-bais* which are used to compose the Torah. This indicates our wish that Hashem deal kindly with us in merit of the righteous who are continually immersed in the study of His Torah (*Tur* 118).

The Format of blessing #48:

1. We fulfill the special mitzvah of loving and praying for

the righteous.

2. We pray that the righteous will be awarded the best of everything.

> Our Sages teach us that the next best thing to being a Torah Sage is to be close to a Torah Sage!

3. We pray that we merit to always be linked to them. (Our Sages teach us in many places that the next best thing to being a Torah Sage is to be close to a Torah Sage!)

We pray for assistance in fulfilling the obligation to always cling to Torah Sages. For Example: males pray to marry the daughter of a Torah Sage, while females pray to marry a Torah Sage, share meals with them, and to be able to join them in every possible way. (Rambam, *Deos* 6:2).

Bracha #49
The Gift of Jerusalem

...בָּרוּךְ אַתָּה ה' בּוֹנֶה יְרוּשָׁלָיִם.

"...Blessed are You, Eternal Master, Builder of Jerusalem."

It is well known that we are all influenced by our environment. Thus we pray for the holy city of Yerushalayim which was permeated with *kedusha* and perfection, and it transformed and elevated all who entered its gates.

The Gemara (*Megillah* 17b) explains that this blessing follows the previous blessing regarding the righteous, because in Yerushalayim the power and glory of the righteous can flourish unhampered.

When we pray for Hashem's mercy for the righteous and ask to have our lot placed with them forever, we have an underlying purpose. We are fulfilling the precept of "You shall cling to Hashem" (*Devarim* 10:20), i.e., to always be with Hashem by means of joining with genuine Torah scholars whose lives exemplify the ideals and actions of the Torah.

"Arise, shine forth (Zion, the perfect city), your light has arrived, the glory of Hashem will shine on you..."

This bracha emphasizes that we pray to join the righteous in the ideal setting of Hashem's city, Yerushalayim, where Hashem's presence will be evident in the most magnificent manner. "Arise, shine forth (Zion, the perfect city), your light has arrived, the glory of Hashem will shine on you..." (*Yeshaya* 60:1).

The *Tur* (118) points out that the 24 words in this blessing correspond to the 24 letters in the *pasuk* concerning

Hashem's rebuilding of Yerushalayim; *"Bonei Yerushalayim Hashem, nidchei Yisrael yichanes"* (*Tehillim* 147).

Why do the *Tur* and other commentators repeatedly show us how each and every word of our prayers corresponds to great lessons? The obvious answer is that when we pray we should be aware that we are addressing the Master of the Universe and, thus, each word we utter must be prepared to be meaningful, precise and appropriate, as much as possible.

Bracha #50
The Gift of Salvation

...בָּרוּךְ אַתָּה ה׳ מַצְמִיחַ קֶרֶן יְשׁוּעָה.

"Blessed are You, Eternal Master,
Who causes the power of salvation to sprout"

Rashi (*Megillah* 17b) states that the three blessings—for the gathering of all the Jews [#10], the building of Yerushalayim [#14], and the sprout of Dovid [#15]—combine to form a unit of prayers asking for the complete Redemption. We understand that blessings 11 through 13

Bracha #15 of Shemoneh Esrei

are also related, since they refer to those people who deserve to be redeemed and to our leaders.

We now concentrate on the completion of our salvation through the leadership of King Dovid's offspring. Without the proper leaders we are like sheep walking in darkness. Hashem provides us with genuine Torah leaders who can guide us and direct us in every aspect of our lives.

> Who is the author of *Tehillim* and the man behind the system of 100 daily brachos? Dovid Hamelech. The connection is obvious. In both Dovid teaches us how to devote our lives to praising Hashem.

We mention here that elevating Moshiach's power is the equivalent of Hashem's salvation, which we yearn for all the time. This highlights the purpose of a Jewish king. The king's role is to teach us how to serve Hashem properly. The greater the Jewish king, the more we will learn how to truly serve Hashem.

"Dovid, Your Servant"

King Dovid was the Al-mighty's servant *par excellence*. All of Dovid's desires and efforts were dedicated solely to the service of Hashem. His self-effacement was perfect to the degree that we conclude this blessing without even mentioning his name again. The purpose of the Jewish king was to enforce Hashem's Torah. The distinction between the king and all the other leaders we pray for in Bracha #11 of Shemoneh Esrei is that the other leaders teach Hashem's Torah and His ways. The king, however, also coordinated the fulfillment, practice and implementation of all the laws of the Torah.

The previous blessing also concludes with a plea for the return of the royal throne of Dovid, but there we referred to it as part of the structure of the city of Yerushalayim. Here, we allude to Dovid's overall power; he serves as G-d's agent in order to teach us to relate to Hashem in each and everything we do.

Hope to You

As we end this bracha we state — "We hope all day to You for salvation." The *Shulchan Aruch* (118), in *Shaarei Teshuva*, teaches us two thoughts we should focus on at this point.

The obligation of yearning for salvation is so great that the Gemara (*Shabbos* 31a) warns that at the future judgement we will be asked six questions and one of them is — "Did you hope for salvation?"

Additionally, Hashem's salvation occurs at many intervals throughout the day. We have to keep hoping to Him for help for all of our small and large needs.

Bracha #51
Gift of Hashem's Attention

בָּרוּךְ אַתָּה ה' שׁוֹמֵעַ תְּפִלָּה.

"...Blessed are You, Eternal Master, Who hears prayers."

Bracha #16 of Shemoneh Esrei

Hashem listens to our prayers. What an amazing privilege! Whenever we have a problem, we are encouraged to speak to the Master of the universe. We have a special "800" number, no telephone bill at the end of the month, the line is never busy, we always get through on the first sincere try, and the *Abishter* is always listening to us—even in the middle of the night.

One of the great privileges of the Jewish nation is the right every Jew has to speak directly to Hashem, as it says:

"How beloved are Jews, for they do not require an intermediary!" (*Yoma* 52a).

Our privilege carries with it the responsibility to develop the awareness that when we pray we are indeed conversing with the Al-mighty, and that He is actually listening to our voice and thoughts.

This prayer is the culmination of the middle prayers of the Shemoneh Esrei and it summarizes the requests for all of our personal and communal needs. We are now asking that Hashem listen to and respond to all of our above requests.

> **This is our opportunity to focus on any and all of our needs to tell Hashem, Who is always listening and eager to respond!**

Now is the time to also think of any other specific personal needs that were not mentioned yet:

ههه Do you or your children need a *shidduch?* This is an opportune time to pray for yourself and for others in need as well! ("Listen to *our* voices" — shema koleinu.)

ههه Do you need spiritual, physical, or financial help? Pray for yourself and others.

ههه Are you worried about your children? Now's the perfect time to pray for them.

The significance of this bracha is emphasized in a halacha in *Shulchan Aruch, Orach Chayim*, 109:1 – The amen of the third and sixteenth blessings (both conclude their respective sections of the Shemoneh Esrei) are equally important regarding certain technical laws. We have to realize that this is our opportunity to focus on any and all of our needs to address Hashem who is *always listening and eager to respond!*

Bracha #52
Gift of Hashem's Favor

בָּרוּךְ אַתָּה ה' הַמַּחֲזִיר שְׁכִינָתוֹ לְצִיּוֹן.

"…Blessed are You, Eternal Master, Who returns His Presence to Zion."

᳀ ᳀ ᳀

As we conclude the Shemoneh Esrei, this bracha is the first of the group of three brachos dealing with our preparation to take leave of Hashem.

Bracha #17 of Shemoneh Esrei

This bracha consists of five parts:

1. Favor us and our prayers—We request that Hashem should willingly accept all of the prayers we have mentioned.

2. Restore the *Avodah*—We yearn to also bring actual *korbonos at the Bais HaMikdash,* instead of merely offering a substitute of prayer.

3. And the fire offerings—There are different opinions concerning whether this phrase is connected to the above phrase or to the phrase that follows. An offering on the fire symbolizes our complete devotion and sacrifice to Hashem.

4. May we always find *favor*—We repeat the word *rotzon* three times here to indicate that it is our dearest wish in life to find favor in the eyes of the Al-mighty.

5. May our eyes view the return of the *Shechina*... – This phrase sums up the theme of this great blessing—Our desire to come closer to Hashem, and to merit being in His presence!

Prayer with Love

We emphasize here that our prayer is expressed with love. We love to pray because prayer is a concrete method of expressing our devotion to Hashem (*Praise My Soul*, Rabbi Avigdor Miller, pg. 436).

Eyes to Hashem

"May our eyes view..." In order for our eyes to be able to see holiness, we must guard them from viewing unclean and immoral sights which desensitize the eyes to the spiritual truths regarding service of Hashem. In a sense we can compare our eyes to a camera. If we waste film on silly pictures we won't have any left for memorable occasions.

Keep in Mind

Whenever we pray to bring offerings, it is as if we are actually performing these great mitzvos even though we are in exile. (When one truly desires to do a mitzvah, but is unable to do so, it is considered as if one actually performed it! [*Brachos* 6a])

Bracha #53
The Gift of Thanks

...בָּרוּךְ אַתָּה ה׳ הַטּוֹב שִׁמְךָ וּלְךָ נָאֶה לְהוֹדוֹת.

"...Blessed are You, Eternal Master, For Your name is "Good"
and to You it is pleasant to give thanks."

"We thank (*modim*) You."

The Hebrew word "*modim*" ("מודים") has a gematria of

**Bracha #18 of
Shemoneh Esrei**

100. This is an indication of our obligation
to give thanks to Hashem at least one hundred times every day (*Kol Bo, siman* 122).
"We thank You" for everything because it
is all from You.

"One who says *Modim* properly is considered to have ful-
filled all 100 brachos!" (*Daas Zekeinim Baalei HaTosfos,
Devarim* 10:12)

Avos Repeat

This blessing (*Modim*) is one which parallels the first
bracha of Shemoneh Esrei. That is why we refer here to
Hashem as "Our G-d and the G-d of our [three] fathers." Just

as we began our prayer with an awareness of the *avos* who taught us the truth of Hashem, so, too, we begin *Modim* with the awareness that our fathers taught us that Hashem is the owner/creator/controller/and provider of all benefits!

This explanation fits well with the opinion quoted in the *Mishna Berurah* (101:3), that *Modim* is on the same level as the bracha of *Avos*. When saying each of these brachos there is an essential requirement—concentration. Regarding the bracha of *Avos*, the Gemara says one who fails to think about what he is saying does *not* fulfill his obligation to recite Shemoneh Esrei. In addition, one is obligated to bow down at the beginning and at the end of both of these brachos.

Thanking Hashem is such a basic fundamental in our lives that the first word a Jew expresses upon waking every morning is מודה אני "Thank You…" (*Alei Shur* vol. 2:285).

Thank You List

We now itemize some general categories of benefits that motivate us to offer our gratitude to Hashem, each of which includes millions of items:

1. **We thank Hashem for our lives**—including everything that keeps us alive—our brain, heart, lungs, stomach, two kidneys, the liver, two hands, two feet, nose, two eyes, two ears, mouth, and countless other organs and body parts

that facilitate human life.

2. **We also offer thanks for our souls** — each of our souls is a Divine spiritual entity that gives life to our body. It is the essence of who we are. It is the source of the unlimited potential greatness that lies within each and every one of us. We must thank Hashem especially for returning our soul to us daily. The Medrash explains that if you were greatly in debt to someone and then you gave him something of value for safekeeping, he would keep it as collateral. But each and every morning Hashem keeps returning our *neshama* to us.

> Every day when you mouth the word "modim" in your davening, visually imagine one specific item for which you are thanking Hashem now!

3. **We thank Hashem for miracles** — many of which come our way constantly, although we often fail to recognize them (Rashi, *Shabbos* 13b).

We Always Put Our Hope in You

Now is the time to pause to reflect about these words of prayer to Hashem, in order to be sincere and truthful while stating that, "We always put our hope in You." (Ask yourself: What do I hope for and request from Hashem daily? And answer — good health, good food, family and friends who like me, etc.)

All the Living Praise You

The implication here is that the basic gift of being alive requires thanks on our part, in and of itself. The *Shulchan Aruch* (*siman* 119:1) says that the word **חיים** — *chaim* — serves to remind us of four situations in which a person must thank and praise Hashem:

ח — חבוש — One who was released from prison,

י — יסורים — One who was healed from illness,

י — ים — One who survived an ocean voyage,

מ — מדבר — One who crossed a desert.

Here is a checklist to get you started for the next 20 prayers. Imagine thanking Hashem for your: brain, eyes, ears, hair, nose, fingers, elbows, knees, toes, chin, stomach, kidneys, thighs, heart, lungs, intestines, blood circulation, digestion, nails and tongue.

Ongoing Life = Ongoing Thanks

"One who is alive shall praise You" (*Yeshaya* 38:19).

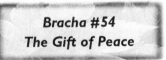

Bracha #54
The Gift of Peace

בָּרוּךְ אַתָּה ה' הַמְבָרֵךְ אֶת עַמּוֹ יִשְׂרָאֵל בַּשָּׁלוֹם...

"...Blessed are You, Eternal Master,
Who blesses His people Israel with peace."

ෂ ෂ ෂ

"Peace is the ultimate container of all blessings" (*Oktzin* 3:12).

Bracha #19 of Shemoneh Esrei

Every single prayer request we make must be tempered and balanced to coincide with all of the other parts of our lives. An intellectual genius who is unable to get along with others or a wealthy person who has cancer are examples of imbalanced individuals who are limited in the benefits they derive from their talents or achievements.

We pray for all-encompassing peace/*shalom*. Peace is so unique and all inclusive it is even considered one of Hashem's names! Peace refers to the harmony of fulfillment that renders one a true success. We want everything from Hashem, but only in its proper measure, so that we may achieve our fullest potential in all aspects of perfection. We need our health, wealth, and spiritual growth to develop in a balanced way.

Conclusion

To reach the heights of prayer is a task to which our lives are dedicated. There is so much profundity in this endeavor that every day we must strive to apply ourselves to this study to the best of our ability. This brief work is merely an outline to direct us to more thought in our prayers.

Rav Chaim Volozhiner writes that since the words of our prayers were prepared by the Sages of the Great Assembly — comprised of one hundred and twenty of the greatest Sages — including Ezra the scribe and some of the other last prophets, we understand that the profundity of these brachos and prayers surpasses even the *Mishnayos.* "Each time we pray we are able to achieve accomplishments in the cosmos… Every prayer from the beginning of time until Moshiach's arrival is unique and accomplishes special improvements in the world" (*Nefesh HaChaim* 2:13).

The above nineteen prayer blessings are repeated in the Shemoneh Esrei of Mincha: Blessings 55-73, and the Shemoneh Esrei of Maariv: Blessings 74-92 with each of these prayers having a total of these same nineteen blessings.

Blessings for a Meal

*T*he only *bracha* of the 100 daily blessings that every commentator agrees is a Torah law (*d'Oraysa*) is that of Birchas Hamazon. We say this blessing to thank Hashem after we eat a meal which includes bread.

> **Bracha #93**
> **The Gift of Hands**

בָּרוּךְ אַתָּה ה׳ אֱלֹקֵינוּ מֶלֶךְ הָעוֹלָם
אֲשֶׁר קִדְּשָׁנוּ בְּמִצְוֹתָיו, וְצִוָּנוּ עַל נְטִילַת יָדָיִם:

"Blessed are You, Eternal Master, our G-d, King of the universe, Who commanded us regarding the washing of our hands."

We make this blessing before we eat any bread. In it we express our gratitude to Hashem for providing us with hands with which we can hold the food and thus eat in a comfortable position. We wash our hands for two reasons.

> Our hands contain over 1,000 nerve endings. This enables them to detect sensations of heat, cold, pain, size, shape & texture.

The first is in order to clean them in a physical way and the second reason symbolizes our spiritual cleanliness and elevation.

"Who will ascend on Hashem's mountain, who can stand on His Holy Hill? One who has clean hands…" (*Tehillim* 24).

When we abstain from unclean activities, when we limit the use of the hands Hashem provides us with to activities that Hashem allows, we become sanctified. Although one can fulfill his handwashing with a minimal amount of water (*reviis*), one should try to use an abundance of water in honor of Hashem. One who does so will merit a full measure of wealth from Hashem (*Shulchan Aruch, Orach Chaim* 158:10).

The First Bracha of Bentching

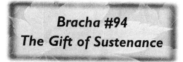

Bracha #94
The Gift of Sustenance

...בָּרוּךְ אַתָּה ה' הַזָּן אֶת הַכֹּל:

"...Blessed are You, Eternal Master, Who sustains all."

❦ ❦ ❦

The *nusach* (wording) of the first bracha in *bentching* was formulated by Moshe Rabbeinu, when the Jews received the *mann* (food from heaven) during their stay in the desert (*Brachos* 48b). This heavenly food, provided to us in Moshe's merit (because of his righteousness and prayers), teaches us monumental lessons; namely, "that man does not live by bread alone" (*Devarim* 8:3). If Hashem desired to sustain us by having us eat wood, we could! It is Hashem's will that allows us to be maintained on the manner of fare He created.

The Mann

Not only was the substance of the *mann* miraculous, so was the entire method of its deliverance for forty years.

Imagine one day opening your door on the way to work and finding an envelope at your feet containing a hundred dollars. You may take the day off. The following day, you are once again on the way to work, when lo and behold, you find a similar envelope. Once again you spend your day learning. When this continues to occur daily, you realize that you can quit your job and spend all your time learning!

We have to realize that, in a hidden manner, each of us is still being supplied by Hashem with sustenance as miraculous as the *mann*.

"The miracle of food (the process by which Hashem causes a seed to transform earth into food) which Hashem provides us with is as spectacular as the miracle of the splitting of the sea" (*Pesachim* 118a).

❧ ❧ ❧

This first bracha of *bentching* can be divided into five segments (perhaps paralleling the Five Books of the Torah).

Introduction to Bentching

The introduction to *bentching* is similar to every blessing.

ברוך — Blessed. The word ברוך comes from the root word, ברך "knee," alluding to bending the knee. Although we do not actually bend our knees each time we make a blessing, ברוך signifies our humble gratitude.

אתה ה׳ — You, L-rd. When we make a blessing, we must

be cognizant of Whom we are addressing. Hashem is the Master of everything. He was always, He is now, and He will continue to be always.

אלקינו — our G-d. This word indicates justice. Hashem is in control, the source of all power and energy. He provides precise compensation for all deeds and misdeeds.

מלך העולם — King of the universe. He is in complete control of everything.

Part I

הזן את הכל — He sustains the entire world. Not only has Hashem created the world, but Hashem continually sustains the world, maintaining its existence day by day, moment by moment.

The three words הזן את הכל sufficiently describe the concept of this entire blessing. However, to develop our appreciation of the magnitude of Hashem's kindness we elaborate on this theme in the text of the blessing.

Why do we thank Hashem for *sustaining the world*? Why not just thank Hashem for supplying us with our personal needs by the meal we just ate?

This reminds us of the story told of a child born in captivity in a dungeon. All he knows of the world is the dungeon he inhabits, and, therefore, he is not distressed by its conditions. Instead he considers them normal and attempts to learn about them. He notices that every day, someone lowers a bucket with bread and water for his survival. He realizes that a benefactor is lowering his food to him and he is moved to thank him. The next day, he graciously acknowledges his gratitude to the guard who he believes to be the source of his provisions. The guard, however, apprises him of his servile status. The guard is, after all, only a messenger of the king and must do the bidding of his master. The child resolves to express his gratitude to the king and, the next day, asks the guard to convey his deep appreciation to the king for the bread and water that he receives. The guard disdains the child's naivete. Such a sentiment is a denigration in comparison to the king's actual abilities. Is the king so poor that he can only provide bread and water? He supplies so much more to his subjects at large. Such an expression of gratitude would belittle the king's capabilities.

Similarly, we cannot simply thank Hashem for *our* food. We must acknowledge the vastness of His power to give all that is vital to every creature in the entire universe.

A—כולו—every part of the whole. Not only does Hashem provide for the world, He alone provides for the *entire* world. There are no other sources except Hashem's goodness. Without Him, there would be no sustenance.

B—בטובו—with all of His goodness. Hashem not only gives us everything we require, He does so with immense

> **Even if we are without merit, Hashem furnishes our needs and some of our wants.**

kindness. Our food is tasty, healthy, appealing to the eye, and aromatic. There are limitless ways to prepare the same food and different sources for the same nutrients so that we can choose to our taste and heart's content. This variety serves to teach us a little about the goodness of Hashem and His unlimited greatness and kindness.

C—בחן—with grace (related to חנם—for nothing). Even if one cannot afford to pay, even if we are without merit, Hashem furnishes our needs and wants. For example, Hashem provides edible fruits and vegetables in the wild which we could just go pick and eat. Hashem also provides plentiful wells and streams full of clear clean water. When a farmer plants grain what does he pay Hashem to make the wheat grow? Hashem provides all of us with food—through farmers who get paid for their efforts—but who pays Hashem?

D—בחסד—with kindness. Hashem provides us with what we need in abundance. He could give us only the bare minimum. Trees and fruit grow with thousands of seeds contained within them which can then produce more crops. In addition, Hashem grants the requirements for each of his creations at every stage of their development. As we say in *Ashrei*:

"The — "עיני כל אליך ישברו, ואתה נותן להם את אכלם בעתו" eyes of all hope to You, and You give them their food in its time."

At each phase of life, various forms of food and tastes are required. Hashem provides a most marvelous medium for dispensing a baby's essentials, special milk that is formulated distinctly for each species. As the baby ages, different consistencies of food are made available.

ובֿרחמים—E—and with mercy. Even to those who are undeserving. The root of this word, רחם (*rechem*), means womb, and refers to a mother's mercy. A child does not have to earn his or her mother's affection. A mother provides for her child even without justification—Hashem has implanted in her a love for her baby. This is an example of Hashem's love and compassion to all of His creations.

Part II of the First Bracha

הוא—He. We are often misled by Hashem's various agents who seem to bring us what we need causing us to fail to note the force behind them all.

For example, when we eat bread — even though it was the farmer who toiled to till the ground and harvest the wheat, the miller who worked to mill the flour, and the baker who spent time transforming the flour and water into bread — the *source* of the chain and each and every step of the bread-making procedure stems from Hashem's goodness.

> The source of the chain and each and every step of the bread-making procedure stems from Hashem's goodness.

נותן — gives. This word implies it is given as a gift, out of Hashem's generosity, without His being coerced for any reason.

לחם — bread. Previously, we thanked Hashem for nourishing the entire world, but we did not mention bread specifically. However, if we leave things in the abstract, it is difficult to appreciate them properly; thus we focus on thanking Hashem for the specific details of His gifts — the very bread we eat.

לכל בשר — to all living creatures. We acknowledge that Hashem provides each living creature with that which most specifically benefits them. Some animals eat grass and others vegetation; some eat insects; and some eat other creatures. Each one fulfills a certain niche in an ecological system Hashem has designed.

כי לעולם חסדו—because His kindness endures forever. How does the food which sustains our flesh last forever? All material substances have a spiritual counterpart, which provides us with everlasting nurturing. Food enables us to live and perform mitzvos. Mitzvos then provide us with a portion in the World to Come, which is eternal.

Five Spiritual Tests

When we deal with food there are five spiritual tests we confront:

1) We must ascertain if the food we are about to eat is kosher.

2) We need to consider if we are making the blessings properly, both before and after we eat the food. While saying these blessings we have to sincerely concentrate on having our authentic gratitude for the food.

> Hashem provides each living creature with that which most specifically benefits them.

There are superb examples of how to feel gratitude—Rav Simcha Zissel Ziv of Kelm, for example, would first take a look outside his window at a patch of earth before he recited the blessing for bread. He did this to appreciate the con-

trast between the earth and the wheat which Hashem causes to grow from the earth which results in bread.

3) We must make sure we refrain from overeating or eating when not permitted.

4) We must remember our responsibility to share our
food with the needy when possible.

5) Whenever we eat, it is important to remember to eat
l'shaim Shamayim, for the sake of heaven, i.e., we should eat
with the purpose of maintaining our physical needs so that
we stay healthy in order to be able to serve Hashem.

Part III of the First Bracha

ובטובו הגדול—and in His great goodness. Although
Hashem's goodness has been previously mentioned, we
emphasize here the constant and unlimited nature of His
goodness.

תמיד—constantly. Not only has Hashem given us sustenance in the past, He continues to do so, without missing
even one day.

לא חסר לנו—we have never lacked. This is similar to the
verse in Psalm 23: "ה' רועי לא אחסר—Hashem is my
provider. I shall not lack." Simply put, it means that whatever food we eat daily we have because of Hashem.

Hashem provides abundance to the world at large.

Scientists agree that if the whole world worked together to feed mankind, there would be plenty for everyone. Hashem, however, built this world with a system of reward and punishment, which means that all of mankind is expected to keep the seven mitzvos of Bnei Noach in order to maintain the minimum standard of decency. If they did that and abolished idolatry, bloodshed, immorality, stealing, etc. people would realize that they can provide the basics for everyone from Hashem's abundant supplies!

People however utilize or misutilize their free will and choose all kinds of problems which puts the world into the state of affairs we witness where we have millions of people around the world suffering from hunger. As it says in *Tehillim*, "we will not lack if we follow *tzedek* and Hashem will be with us." This point is further clarified in Bereishis. In the beginning of the Chumash, Hashem made everything good. As a result of sin, lack and deprivation were introduced.

How do we relate to this verse nowadays? The answer is that Hashem is compared to a shepherd who not only brings his flock to graze, but He knows when they have had enough and may overdo it.

Similarly, parents stop children from overindulging in sweets. The child may feel deprived, but we are aware that it is truly in his or her own best interest.

Once we realize that Hashem always takes care of us, we understand that even when we seem to lack something, it is in our own best interest! We may, however, not understand Hashem's purpose. The purpose may be to teach us to pray to Hashem for food, or that Hashem wants the person to make some *hishtadlus* (effort) on his or her own behalf.

> **Since Hashem always takes care of us, even when we seem to lack something, it is in our own best interest!**

Even when the Jews received *mann* for 40 years in the desert, it did not land right in their mouths or hands. Every morning they had to collect it (*Shemos* 16, 21), and it was perishable. If they attempted to leave any *mann* until the next morning, it would rot. (Except for Shabbos, when they were instructed to keep the leftovers from Friday.) Why is it that this most heavenly food was designed to spoil in one day? In order to teach and train the Jews to seek their sustenance every day by prayer from Hashem (*Yoma* 76a).

"The daily falling of the *mann* from the sky was as miraculous as the falling of rain. Both are Hashem's deeds. Everything in nature is actually under Hashem's complete control, which means one thing: kindliness" (*Rejoice O*

Youth, Rabbi Avigdor Miller, par. 869).

Part IV of the First Bracha

ואל יחסר לנו מזון לעולם ועד—and let us not lack food forever. The position of this request follows the general system of prayer, which can be compared to how a servant would approach his master (*Brachos* 34a). First the servant praises his master, then he makes his request. The servant concludes his request by once again thanking and praising his master. The preceding part was our praise to Hashem; now we state our request. We also conclude our request with a justification for our plea.

בעבור שמו הגדול—for the sake of His great name. Why should Hashem consent to provide us with sustenance? Are we deserving or have we earned His continuous support? Rather we ask Him to comply with our request for the sake of His name. This is similar to our request in the prayers recited during the ten Days of Awe, from Rosh Hashanah until Yom Kippur. Part of our "not sinning" includes our acknowledgement of Hashem as the source of all food by praying to Hashem for our food and by obeying His Torah.

זכרנו לחיים...למענך אלקים חיים—Remember us for life...for Your sake. We ask Hashem to comply with our requests for an assortment of reasons that are included in "for the sake of

His great name", among them:

1) So that we may continue to serve Him. We beg Hashem to provide us with our needs, for without them we cannot fulfill our obligations to Him.

2) So that we will always appreciate that He is the source of our salvation. This means He helps us to stay alive every day, He helps us stay healthy and He helps us in every way we need to be successful. We desire to continue to recognize Hashem's greatness and goodness. As Hashem continues to supply us with good things, we are motivated to continually praise and thank Him.

3) In order to inspire others also to praise Hashem by making them aware of the bounty that He has in store for those who follow His ways.

It is only with these reasons that we justify our continued existence and our request for sustenance.

Rabbi Miller writes that when we learn to be aware of our Creator we achieve the greatest good which food provides for us (*Sing, You Righteous*, p. 509).

Part V of the First Bracha

כי הוא — because He is.

We now return to praising Hashem. We emphasize that הוא, He, is the one Who provides. Although there are many intermediaries—all G-d-sent—who play a part in delivering our sustenance, ultimately, there is only one Source.

Learning to be aware of our Creator is the greatest benefit which food provides for us

When we attend a banquet, it is considered polite and appropriate to thank the waiter who serves us our food and drink. But we are quite aware that it is not through his generosity that we are enjoying a sumptuous repast. We understand that it is our host who has provided us with the meal and has paid the staff to serve us. If we are even more discerning, we realize that even our host is only a distributor of this largess—for the true bestower of all goodness is Hashem.

Similarly, we can become aware that if we are blessed with a generous boss, a booming business, or a munificent benefactor—although we must express our gratitude to them—they are simply the emissaries carrying out the will of Hashem, the Sole Provider.

קל—the Source of all energies, the Master of all forces.

זן—Who provides all nourishment. All of Hashem's forces are dedicated to supplying nourishment. This is a novel thought. In his books, Rav Avigdor Miller, *shlita*, explains that the purpose of everything that Hashem does in this world is to provide the world with its food supply. This is why the sun shines, the winds blow, and the force of gravity exists. All of nature cooperates in manufacturing the world's food.

> Our stomachs can digest the toughest materials with a powerful acid, which miraculously does not destroy the lining of our stomach cavities!

Rav Saadya Gaon was asked whether or not these components of nature would exist after *techiyas hameisim* (the resurrection of the dead). He replied that all these are only necessary for the world as it exists today, because this is a food-world. In the World to Come we will receive rewards from Hashem in a sublime way and the system will be different.

ומפרנס לכל—apportions to all. Hashem could have merely produced food and left it up to the individual to get it. But He does much more. He also serves as the world's administrator and apportions the food properly. As the *pasuk* in *Tehillim* says (*Psalms* 145:16):

"פותח את ידך ומשביע לכל חי רצון" Hashem (actively) opens His hand to satisfy the desires of all the living.

We are taught that reciting *Ashrei* (Psalm 145) three times daily guarantees that one will merit the World to Come (*Brachos* 46). What makes *Ashrei*'s verses so significant?

The Gemara (*Brachos* 4b) addresses the source of *Ashrei's* uniqueness. The verses, the Gemara says, follow the order of the *Aleph-Bais*, insuring that we use every form of expression possible to praise Hashem. Secondly, *Ashrei* contains the above verse from *Psalms* 145:16. What is the great significance of "Hashem opens His hand to satisfy every life?" The preceding verse (*Psalms* 145:15) already states: " עיני כל אליך ישברו, ואתה נותן להם את אכלם בעתו", "All eyes hope to You and You give them their food in a timely fashion." The following *pasuk* follows this theme, but it adds that we should comprehend that Hashem goes *all out* (so to speak) in this effort. His efforts on our behalf are of unlimited magnitude! He uses His entire hand and all of His immense power! Thus we understand that we must praise Hashem for everything He does for us, for His unlimited kindness is dedicated to us.

Some say the word זן (nourishes) refers to Hashem's supplying us with food, while מפרנס (sustains) refers to clothing and, according to *Aitz Yosef,* ומטיב (does good) refers to shelter.

> It is Hashem Who sets a plentiful table in front of every individual.

ומטיב לכל—and He is good to all. Here we emphasize Hashem's goodness which is towards *all* the living.

ומכין מזון—and He prepares food. All brachos end with a

synopsis of the theme of the bracha. Here we reiterate that Hashem supplies our needs.

לכל בריותיו — for all His creatures.

The fact that Hashem prepares food for us is illustrated in the *Gemara* (*Kiddushin* 32b) which discusses whether it is proper for a great *talmid chochom* to serve as a waiter to others. Rabon Gamliel considered it appropriate. After all, he notes, even Avraham Avinu — the greatest personality of his time, devoted his life to serving others.

Rabbi Tzadok asks: Why do we bring this proof from a person and ignore Hashem's prestige? After all, Hashem is continuously and personally involved in serving all His creations. He causes the winds to blow to transport the clouds which water the fields through rain, which in turn causes the plants to grow. Thus it is Hashem Who sets a plentiful table in front of every individual. Surely we must emulate His ways! (*Kiddushin* 32b). The Torah teaches us "you shall walk in His ways."

The bentching continues: אשר ברא — which He created. In order for us to gain the awareness that Hashem desires kindliness, He created people. In this way He has recipients upon whom to bestow His bounty. Thus He sets an example of how we should live our lives in search of doing acts of kindness to others.

We should search for people to bestow benefits upon. It is obvious that we should help those who come knocking on our doors for help. In emulation of Hashem we go further to take the initiative to look for those in need of help.

ברוך אתה ה' — Blessed are You Hashem,

הזן את הכל — Who sustains all. We began first with the words, הזן את העולם — Who feeds the world. Now, we change the terminology to הזן את הכל — Who feeds all.

We do this because there is a difference between a superficial notion about Hashem's ways and a deeper consideration based on a study of Hashem's benefits to us. At first we are more abstract, discussing how Hashem feeds the whole world; now, after delving into the subject we zero in on "He feeds all."

How did Avraham Avinu bring people closer to Hashem? He first served them an abundant meal for which they felt grateful. When his guests attempted to thank him, Avraham explained that he could not accept all of their thanks since he was only a servant of the house. When his guests requested the opportunity to thank the Master of the House, Avraham taught them about Hashem—the true

We are obligated to ponder the source of our sustenance and explore our obligation to express our gratitude.

155

Master (*Sotah* 10b). If they refused to believe in Hashem, Avraham would ask for payment for the meal—a substantial sum as befits the difficulties of providing such a vast meal in the remote area where he lived. We can imagine that most people would reconsider their position until they acknowledged that indeed there is only One Supplier to all creatures.

Was this merely a trick on Avraham's part? No. He was following Hashem's way; Hashem first provides us with food and then asks us to give thanks. The best way to educate people who are physical and spiritual is to utilize the physical to stimulate their spiritual recognition. Before eating, only a short blessing is required, because we do not have the patience to think about the significance of what we are eating when we are starved. However, once our hunger has been satisfied and we have eaten our fill, we are obligated to ponder the source of our sustenance and explore our obligation to express our gratitude. When we begin reciting the first blessing of *bentching*, we consider that Hashem sustains the whole world. However, after elaborating on the benefits for the world-at-large, we conclude with

> Reciting a bracha mechanically without thought is like paying with a counterfeit coin.

"He feeds all," which is a more concrete emphasis of Hashem's kindness to individuals.

"Whoever benefits from this world without a bracha is like one who trespasses by misusing sacred property" (*Brachos* 35b). Rabbi Avigdor Miller notes that this requires more than lip-service; the genuine coin of payment for using this world is a true awareness of the Creator's ownership and kindliness. Reciting a bracha mechanically without thought is like paying with a counterfeit coin. One who eats a meal without concluding with sincere heartfelt thanks to the Creator, owner and supplier, is not merely a thief, but is frustrating the entire purpose of the meal, which is to bring people to the great accomplishment and happiness of becoming more aware of and acknowledging the Creator (*Sing, You Righteous*, Rabbi Avigdor Miller, pg. 352, par. 807).

Bracha #95
The Gift of the Land

נוֹדֶה לְךָ ה' אֱלֹקֵינוּ ...

"We thank You, our G-d..."

Yehoshua composed the second bracha of *Birchas*

alive so that we can serve Hashem. Thus we do not simply thank Hashem for the food which keeps us alive; instead we consider the big picture of our life and its purpose.

> Ten is a basic number in Jewish ideology which originates from the ten stages of Creation.

It is significant that we enumerate ten gifts. Ten is a basic number in Jewish ideology and originates from the ten stages of Creation. The number ten is repeated many times: Avraham Avinu passed ten trials to achieve his status as the pillar of the world, ten plagues were sent upon Egypt because they interfered with our mission to serve Hashem. Ten commandments—the ten all-inclusive obligations of the Torah—were given to us so that we maintain the ten stages of creation. Perhaps, even our ten fingers were designed by Hashem to remind us of these ten obligations.

Before we proceed, consider if you were asked to list ten things for which you are most grateful in your life, what would you mention?

Would you be grateful for your life? Food? Your home? Your independence? The country you live in? Would you extend the list to include milestones that highlighted your life? Your graduation which marked the opportunity for your education? Your wedding? The birth of your children?

Hamazon as the Jews entered Eretz Yisroel. Our ancestors always gave thanks for the good land that Hashem had promised them, but a universal text wasn't formulated until the Jews actually settled in Eretz Yisroel, during the days of Yehoshua (*Brachos* 48b).

The Land Connection

What is the connection between the food the Jews ate and the land? When eating a meal for which we are grateful, we must be sure to thank Hashem not only for the food itself, but also for the land He provided which is the actual food-machine enabling the production of such delicious food.

The earth, created and constantly maintained by the Master of the Universe, is the most ancient and most modern food-factory. Place a seed in earth, add water, some fertilizer, and allow it the benefit of Hashem's sunshine, and it will begin the process that will yield flour, with which we can create bread, noodles and 100 other varieties of food....

Thanks Times Ten

Within this second bracha of *Birchas Hamazon*, we find a list of ten things we are grateful for. Why do we thank Hashem for these additional benefits now? Food is never an end in itself—it is a means to achieve our goal. We eat to stay

(These are things we *should* be grateful for, but often, unless we sincerely attempt to sensitize ourselves to continue to be thankful in retrospect, we may fail to adequately express our thanks...) A sensible person who was released from jail with the help of an individual, would surely be grateful to his benefactor for the rest of his life! Keep these in mind and compare them to the list that our Sages compiled in this second bracha of *Birchas Hamazon*.

נודה לך — We thank You.

This bracha begins and ends with thanks. The term נודה is similar to the word ידה which means to lift up, to elevate. When we thank Hashem, we are obligated to praise Hashem and to hold Him in high esteem, as the donor of our benefits.

ה' אלקנו — Hashem, the ultimate source of everything.

Benefit I

על שהנחלת לאבותינו — for giving our forefathers this inheritance.

ארץ חמדה — a desirable land. In thanking Hashem for the unique food-machine which Hashem has created to produce food for us, we are grateful that He has not only given us land, but rather the choicest land in the world. Eretz Yisroel is so unique that it was desired by all. Hashem desires it, the Avos desired it, Moshe Rabbeinu desired it, and kings from all over the world made sure to own at least some real estate in this unique land.

טובה ורחבה — a good and spacious land. These two terms are from the *pasuk* in *Shemos* (3:8) which continues...

ארץ זבת חלב ודבש — a land flowing with milk and honey. The land was so rich that milk flowed from the udders of animals, and the dates would drip honey until there were pools of this combined liquid in many areas. Chazal also explain this as a metaphor to describe all of the land's produce, which was as nutritious as the best milk and sweet and tasty as honey.

טובה — denotes quality and ורחבה — denotes quantity. Sometimes we may have excellent food, but an insufficient amount to satiate ourselves. At other times, the food is plentiful, but its quality is mediocre. The land Hashem gave us has the potential to produce the most excellent fruits in abundance. In addition, the Gemara (*Kesubos* 112) teaches that the produce of Eretz Yisroel ripens faster than anywhere else.

Even those Jews who do not yet live in Eretz Yisroel have an inherited ownership right to the land and must therefore thank Hashem for owning a piece of that great land.

Benefit II

ועל שהוצאתנו ה' אלקנו מארץ מצרים — and for taking us out

of the land of *Mitzrayim* (Egypt). Hashem did not just award us the land and leave us to struggle to get there; rather He liberated us from *Mitzrayim* and led us to the land of our inheritance. As we sit back and thank Hashem for our food, we are obligated to also consider *who* is eating the food (our background). Hashem took us out of bondage and, many generations later, we benefit from this meal that He has enabled us now to enjoy.

We say this phrase in first person, because our Sages teach us that "in every generation a person is obligated to imagine as if he himself came out of Egypt" (*Pesachim* 116b).

Benefit III

ופדיתנו מבית עבדים — and He redeemed us from the house of slavery. Had we remained slaves, no matter how favored our lot and our land, we would have been unable to enjoy it fully. A slave does not fully enjoy the land of his master, regardless of how fruitful it may be. It is essential to continually remind ourselves that if Hashem had not redeemed us from slavery, we would still be subservient (*Pesachim* 116b).

Benefit IV

ועל בריתך שחתמת בבשרנו — and for the covenant which you stamped in our flesh. Not only did Hashem provide us our freedom (which He may have done merely out of a desire to help the unfortunate), but He also chose us as His own people. This is a unique privilege given only to *Klal* Yisroel. We are thankful that Hashem has awarded us with a unique badge demonstrating the eternal bond between us. Although the *bris* is stamped on a boy's body when he is eight days old, we keep thanking Hashem for it our entire life.

> Hashem has awarded us with a unique badge demonstrating the eternal bond between us.

There is a concept called למפרע בחירה, a retroactive freewill choice. When we thank Hashem for having a *bris* it is as if we are consenting now to the eternal bond with Hashem. A female is also thankful that she belongs to this great nation and that her father, brothers, husband and sons wear this unique badge of honor.

Benefit V

ועל תורתך—and for Your Torah. Not only has Hashem chosen us as His people, He has also given us a perfect guidebook to teach us how to truly succeed in all of our endeavors. The Torah is the *greatest* of all the gifts that Hashem has bestowed upon us.

שלמדתנו — which You taught us. Hashem *teaches* us His Torah, which implies that we have to listen and learn. To understand the Torah one must exercise effort, and then Hashem aids the person: "which *You* have *taught*" and continue to teach to us. It is as if Hashem participates in our efforts. He is our teacher, as we say in the bracha before we learn Torah:

> **All the world's material things and all the mitzvos of the Torah are not equal to even one single word of Torah.**

המלמד תורה לעמו ישראל — Who teaches Torah to His people, Yisroel.

This benefit is the most important among all the other magnificent gifts that Hashem has bestowed upon us, because Torah study exceeds all other mitzvos. ותלמוד תורה כנגד כולם — Torah study exceeds them all (*Peah* 1).

The *Gemara* (*Yerushalmi, Peah* 1) teaches that all the world's material things and all the mitzvos of the Torah are not equal to even one single word of Torah. This is because the Torah contains the thoughts, the teachings of Hashem, Himself. The Vilna Gaon points out the tremendous accomplishment of one who studies even a few lines of *Gemara*, since it contains many words, each one loaded with such infinite greatness.

תורת ה' תמימה!—Hashem's Torah is perfect! (*Tehillim* 19:8).

Benefit VI

ועל חקיך שהודעתנו—and for Your statutes of which You have informed us. There is a difference between Torah which is "taught" to us and the laws of which Hashem informs us. The Torah contains an assortment of mitzvos, many of which are natural to some degree and understandable to the rational mind. The *chukim*, however, such as *shaatnez* and *kashrus*, defy our understanding, and therefore we are only 'notified' concerning those obligations (*Iyun Tefillah*).

Why are *chukim* listed as a separate category of thanks? Rabbi Avigdor Miller (*Sing You Righteous*, p. 795) notes that it is because there are many additional benefits we derive from these laws. For instance:

1) We receive additional reward for doing these particular mitzvos because:

A. *Chukim* are followed for their own sake (*lishmah*), without an ulterior motive. The reason for practicing them is not because they seem moral, as, for example, honoring one's parents because it is the proper thing to do. Thus, while honoring one's parents, one may forget that it is also important to be motivated by the Heavenly commandment to honor parents and *not* merely by our human understanding.

B. These mitzvos may be more difficult to perform at times if others ridicule us, or if our own Yetzer Hora attempts to dissuade us from following these *chukim,* claiming that these laws are incomprehensible.

2) We gain from not knowing the reasons for *chukim* because we are protected from making erroneous excuses to rationalize them by attempting to apply the reasons to unique situations. When we think we understand something we tend to apply our own feelings to try to bend and twist applications at times.

3) *Chukim* (like *all* other Torah laws) protect our health and safety. Each mitzvah guides us to living a healthy life. For example, keeping Shabbos, a day of rest, is healthy for the body and provides many educational benefits. We have time to think, meditate, reflect on the fact that Hashem created the world in six days and rested on the seventh.

4) All Torah laws are beneficial to our mental health. They keep us in a comprehensive program, a meaningful system of living that deals with every aspect of our lives.

5) They keep us happy and engaged in positive endeavors. Our sages teach: "Hashem desired to purify Yisroel; thus He increased their Torah and mitzvos..." (*Makkos* 23b).

6) They promote peace. The Torah deals with all issues, including issues between humans and G-d and between one person and another.

> **Every mitzvah keeps us mindful of Hashem.**

7) They teach us to respect good and stay away from harm and evil.

8) Primarily, every mitzvah keeps us mindful of Hashem.

An example of the myriad of lessons included in each Torah law can be seen from an insight by the Vilna Gaon. He explains a symbolic lesson included in the law regarding kosher meat. The Torah law specifies that kosher meat must be from an animal that chews its cud and has split hooves. These types of animals symbolize a person who is satisfied with what he has because an animal that chews its cud redigests and reappreciates what it has without looking for additional food. This is similar to the teaching in *Pirkei Avos* (4:1) "Who is wealthy? He who rejoices with his portion!"

In addition, there are two types of *simonim* (signs) required for an animal to be kosher — the inner (chewing its cud) and the outer (split hooves) — to teach us that we — like these gentle animals — need to be kosher both on our inside and outside.

Thus, when the Vilna Gaon ate meat — aside from all the additional lessons he kept in mind — he always reminded himself to be satisfied with what he had and to be a kosher person in a wholesome way — both internally and externally.

Benefit VII

ועל חיים — and for life. There is an old proverb that people use — "*Abi gezunt!*" — It is enough to be healthy! We must be sincerely thankful for our health and thank Hashem for it many times a day. However, we should also say: "*Abi menn lebt*" — It is enough to be alive! The fact that one is alive, even if one is suffering from illness, is enough to obligate an endless amount of gratitude. Life itself is an astonishing gift from Hashem!

If you were offered $20,000,000 or life, which would you choose?

Rabbi Avigdor Miller advises a simple cure for depression. Walk past a cemetery and ask yourself, "What would those bodies on the other side of the fence give to be in my shoes?"

Benefit VIII

חן — favor. Not only does Hashem grant us life itself —

which is a tremendous benefit—He also bestows favor upon us. חן means to find favor, as we see in *Bereishis* (6:8) ונח מצא חן—and Noach found favor. We also find this in *Megillas Esther* (2:15) where it says: ותהי אסתר נושאת חן—and Esther found favor. Hashem adds abundantly to the bare minimum of keeping us alive.

Benefit IX

וחסד—and for the abundant kindness. *Chesed* indicates that more has been provided, beyond the basic requirements. Hashem's providing *chain* to Noach and Esther meant they were provided with astonishing benefits and miracles, as they were busy coping with perilous and hazardous times. *Chesed* denotes abundance beyond the level of favor.

שחוננתנו—which You have granted us. The root of this word is derived from *chinam*—meaning "for free." Hashem provides benefits to us even when we are not deserving of them.

Benefit X

ועל אכילת מזון—and for the food. Now that we have established that the purpose of life is to serve Hashem, we refer back to the gift of food, the fuel which keeps us alive.

שאתה זן ומפרנס אותנו — that you provide for us and apportion to us. (Similar to the previous bracha).

תמיד — constantly.

בכל יום — every day.

ובכל עת — and at all times. Similar to the verse in Ashrei:

ואתה נותן להם את אכלם בעתו — You give everyone their food in its proper time.

ובכל שעה — and at every hour. The noun שעה (hour) is related to the word ישועה (salvation) and the verb שעה (to turn to) (*Bereishis* 4:5). Each of these words indicates a closeness, a desire to spend time with Hashem. (*Praise, My Soul*, Rabbi Avigdor Miller, p. 577). Hashem's provisions for us are a form of His sharing and spending time with us.

We now summarize and conclude this bracha.

ועל הכל — And for everything, i.e., for all ten items mentioned previously.

ה' אלקינו, אנחנו מודים לך — Hashem, our G-d, we thank You.

ומברכים אותך — and we humble ourselves in gratitude to You.

יתברך שמך בפי כל חי — may Your Name be blessed in the mouths of all the living.

Why do we mention *all of the living*? Because our gratitude to Hashem is so immense that we should feel obligated to inspire everyone we come across to also appreciate the benefits that Hashem bestows upon us all. This concept inspired and prompted Avraham Avinu to bring all the people he met to recognize Hashem.

The words "May Your Name be blessed in the mouths of all the living" are both:

 ✑ a prayer that it should be so in the future,

 ✑ a pledge on our part to teach others and publicize our gratefulness to Hashem,

 ✑ and a pledge to support others who do bless Hashem.

Why do we emphasize the word, "בפי" — in the mouths of? We do this to emphasize that this is the main purpose of our mouth — not just to eat, but to praise the One Who provides our nourishment (Rabbi Miller).

תמיד לעולם ועד — continuously, forever — may Hashem's name be praised forever, in all generations.

ככתוב — as it is written in the Torah.

ואכלת ושבעת וברכת את ה' אלקך — when you eat and are satisfied you shall bless Hashem, your G-d.

על הארץ הטובה אשר נתן לך — for the good land which He has given you. As we mentioned previously, we thank Hashem not only for our food, but also for the food-factory where our food originates — the earth.

ברוך אתה ה' על הארץ ועל המזון — Blessed are You, Hashem,

for the land which produces food.

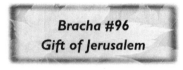

רַחֵם נָא ה' אֱלֹקֵינוּ ...

"Please Have Mercy, Eternal Master, our G-d,..."

This bracha constitutes the end of *bentching d'Oraysa* (by Torah law). We therefore conclude this bracha with amen, even though it is unusual to answer amen to our own bracha.

We began the *bentching* by thanking Hashem for food and for the land. This next bracha's theme is that Hashem should have mercy and rebuild Yerushalayim. We see this from its conclusion, "He Who rebuilds Yerushalayim." Why do we mention this after eating a meal? Because this indicates that we are not just thanking Hashem for the food He provides us — we are also praying for help in achieving the proper purpose of the food — the ultimate goal of our lives — the attainment of spiritual perfection! We therefore ask Hashem to restore the elements necessary to achieve this objective. The land of Eretz Yisroel is not just a promising and desirable land of physical perfection, but, as we mentioned previously, it is also a spiritual entity that is most suited to bringing us closer to Hashem.

The land of Eretz Yisroel is a spiritual entity most suited to bringing us closer to Hashem.

This may be compared to the "prize seat" in a classroom, next to the teacher's desk, where serious students prefer to sit. They realize that this proximity will enable them to achieve their best.

רחם (נא) — (Please) have mercy. The word *rachem* is related to *rechem*, which means womb, since a mother's mercy is boundless and is not dependent on her child's actions. Rather, a mother is moved to an automatic response of mercy by virtue of the fact that the child is her own. Similarly, we ask Hashem to have mercy and help us even if we are unworthy.

ה' אלקינו — Hashem. Our G-d, Who has chosen us as His people.

How to Reach Your Spiritual Heights

We now list five essential components of reaching our spiritual goals of achievement in life:

1. על ישראל עמך — upon Your Jewish nation. The word עמך is related to *imcha*—with you. This means we are asking

Hashem to have mercy on our nation because we always try to be with Him. It is for this reason that we are entitled to ask for mercy.

Three elements are contained in these words:

ఆ On *whom* should Hashem have mercy? On those who are dedicated to Him and consider themselves His people; those who choose to take pride in and identify themselves as members of His Holy Nation. We have chosen to be His servants.

ఆ To *what extent* should Hashem have mercy? To the extent that He should restore us to the level of His people, so that we can fully appreciate His presence.

ఆ *Why* should Hashem have mercy? Because we desire to be His Nation.

2. ועל ירושלים עירך —and on Hashem's city of Yerushalayim. These words contain the same three elements:

> In its glory, Yerushalayim was the consummate city, designed and dedicated for the service of Hashem.

ఆ *What* should Hashem have mercy on? On His city, the city of Yerushalayim.

ఆ To *what extent*? To the extent that it will be restored to its former glory and be recognized as Hashem's chosen city.

ఆ *Why*? Because it is Hashem's city. Yerushalayim

means *Ir sholaim* — the complete and perfect city. In its glory, it was the consummate city, designed and dedicated for the service of Hashem. Today, although we have access to Yerushalayim, it is far from its full measure of holiness. We pray that Hashem should restore it soon to its original perfection.

3. ועל ציון משכן כבודך — and on Tziyon, the dwelling of His Glory. We concentrate on Tziyon, although all of Yerushalayim is holy — because it is the most exceptional spot — the location upon which Hashem has chosen to concentrate His *Shechina*. The word *Shechina* is derived from the word "שכן" — neighbor. Hashem has chosen Tziyon as His dwelling place (so to speak), His capitol city. Although we cannot understand the concept of Hashem residing at a specific site since His essence fills the entire world, yet it cannot be disputed that Tziyon is the place of His choosing. As it says in *Tehillim* (132:13, 14):

כי בחר ה' בציון, אוה למושב לו Hashem has chosen Tziyon, He desires it as His dwelling place.

זאת מנוחתי עדי עד, פה אשב כי אותיה — This is My eternal resting place; here I will dwell for that is My desire.

Therefore we must continually pray for Tziyon to be restored to its original state just as it was when the Bais HaMikdash existed there. We pray that Hashem will once again demonstrate His presence there in an open and glorious manner.

4. ועל מלכות בית דוד משיחך —and for the Kingdom of the house of Dovid. We pray for the restoration of a king from Dovid's lineage, because this, too, is a necessary element for our spiritual perfection; proper leadership is a necessary component to our ultimate success. Dovid's family contains the genes of excellence to bring us to the proper service of Hashem, just as Dovid himself taught us to excel in serving Hashem.

5. ועל הבית הגדול והקדוש —and on the great and holy House. The *Bais HaMikdash* was the vehicle through which Hashem resided within His people. As it says:

ועשו לי מקדש, ושכנתי בתוכם —"you shall make for Me a *Mikdash*, and I will dwell among you" (*Shemos* 25:8).

שנקרא שמך עליו —Upon which your name is called. This is what gives all of the elements their holiness—the fact that they belong to Hashem. We are His people, Yerushalayim is His city, His dwelling place, His home.

> What gives all of the elements their holiness is the fact that they belong to Hashem.

The *Gemara* (*Brachos* 48b) explains that within this bracha, Dovid inserted the reference to *Yisroel Amecha* and

Yerushalayim Irecha. Shlomo added *"Habayis HaGadol Ve'hakodosh"* since he had the merit to build the Bais HaMikdash.

Prayer for Physical Needs

In this section we pray for our physical needs. There's a logic to the placement—we have earned the right to request what we need by demonstrating that we understand our needs' ultimate purpose. We want to utilize our lives to serve Hashem.

אלקינו, אבינו—Hashem, Our Father. The word אב, *Av,* is related to the term אהבה *ahava,* love. A father gives because he loves his children. Hashem's relationship to us is that of a parent to a child.

רענו—care for us, as we find: "ה' רועי לא אחסר"—Hashem is my Shepherd. I shall not lack" (*Psalm* 23:1).

> Hashem does not simply provide us with sustenance; He also guides and enables us to fulfill all of our needs.

A devoted shepherd not only provides his flock with food but is concerned with all of its needs. He makes sure that his sheep are sheltered and protected, that they have sufficient room to graze and water to drink; he makes them as comfortable as possible. Hashem does not simply provide us with sustenance; He also guides and protects us to fulfill all of our needs. We ask Hashem to:

זוננו — provide for us,

פרנסנו — apportion our needs (this includes clothing and shelter),

וכלכלנו — and sustain us. This word contains the word כל, "kol" twice (כל כל). Hashem should provide us with everything, repeatedly, and in abundance.

והרויחנו — and give us "breathing space." Our provisions should be plentiful so that we do not feel "squeezed."

והרוח לנו ה' אלקינו מהרה, מכל צרותינו — Hasten and save us Hashem, Our G-d, from all of our troubles. The word *tzaros* is related to *tzar*, meaning narrow, because problems and stress restrict and confine our ability to function. We ask Hashem to relieve us of these burdens with the term *harvach* — "widen."

We ask Hashem not only for our positive needs but also to remove negative hindrances and afflictions.

(At times, we may attempt to avoid the obligation to *bentch*, by not eating bread. But look at the opportunity that is lost — not only do you lose some of your 100 blessings, you also miss out on the opportunity to pray for relief from *all* of your troubles! Imagine if some benefactor would assure you that he could relieve you of all of your nagging problems, both large and small. He asks you only to voice your requests to him sincerely.)

We now emphasize to Hashem how urgent our request is:

ונא — Please! and now! This is an urgent request.

אל תצריכנו ה' אלקינו — Hashem, don't cause us to need.

לא לידי מתנת בשר ודם — the handouts of human beings.

ולא לידי הלואתם — and not even their loans. Although a loan is less embarrassing to ask for since it is temporary and we plan to repay it, still we prefer not to even need loans.

Why do we include this request at this time?

Imagine if you had dinner in a fancy restaurant and enjoyed the food, but when the bill arrives you wonder if you have sufficient cash. Or perhaps you can use a credit card? The worst case scenario is to be left wondering if the owner will extend credit to you or if the people with you can loan you the money.

Similarly, now that we have come to the end of our meal, we, too, contemplate our ability to pay for it. We ask Hashem that that ability come directly from Him, not through intermediaries.

כי אם לידך — rather let us derive our needs directly from Your hand.

המלאה הפתוחה — which is full and open.

This reminds us of the most important *pasuk* in *Ashrei*, as mentioned before: פותח את ידך ומשביע לכל חי רצון —You open Your hand and satiate the desires of all the living.

What exactly does "Hashem's hand" mean? It represents Hashem's unlimited power, which is full and all encompassing. The entire universe has been created by Him and it is His to give to us. We thus beg Him to do so open-handedly. The more we understand that everything comes from Him the more we trust and the less we will need from others.

הקדושה —His Holy hand. When we accept directly from Hashem, we become sanctified and closer to Him.

והרחבה —generous and unlimited. Hashem's hand is unlimited in every way.

Why are we so concerned to be supported directly by Hashem?

שלא נבוש ולא נכלם —so that we will not be embarrassed or humiliated. The word "נכלם" is related to "כלום" meaning nothing. Someone who is humiliated is made to feel like nothing.

When we accept even a small favor from someone, we become in some small way subservient to that person. *Mishlei* (15:27) teaches: "שונא מתנות יחיה —One who hates gifts shall live." It also says in *Mishlei* (22:7): "עבד לוה לאיש מלוה —a borrower becomes subservient to a lender."

If a lender then asks for a favor, a borrower feels obligated to comply. This interferes with our ability to appreciate Hashem. *Chazal* say that we must focus on being 'עבדי ה, servants of the King—Hashem—*not* a servant of servants (of the King).

לעולם ועד—forever after. This has two meanings:

1. We should *never* suffer shame by needing favors from people throughout our lives.

2. We pray that even in *Olam Habah* we should not suffer shame or humiliation as a result of our needs in this world. One who is not dependent on others for sustenance in this world has a better chance of reaching higher levels of spiritual greatness.

ובנה ירושלים עיר הקודש—and rebuild Yerushalayim, the holy city. At the conclusion of the bracha, we reiterate the main theme.

במהרה בימינו—quickly, in our day. Why is speed of the essence?

1—to restore Hashem's Honor.

2—so that we might live to experience the great joy of having our holy city back and the closeness to Hashem it will engender.

ברוך אתה ה' בונה (ברחמיו) ירושלים אמן—Blessed are You Hashem Who rebuilds Yerushalayim (in His mercy). Amen.

We use the present tense when we thank Hashem here, although Yerushalayim has not yet been fully rebuilt, because we know that Hashem always keeps His word. When we thank Him for doing something even before the act itself becomes evident, we receive a greater reward for demonstrating our faith and belief in Hashem, His desires and abilities (Rav Miller, *Praise My Soul,* pg. 386). In addition, the *pasuk* teaches (*Yirmiya* 17:7):

ברוך הגבר אשר יבטח בה', והיה ה' מבטחו! "Blessed is the person who trusts in Hashem, and Hashem will fulfill his trust."

When we trust that Hashem will provide all of the above we become worthy of deserving to have it come true.

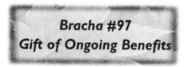

Bracha #97
Gift of Ongoing Benefits

...הטוב והמטיב.

"...Who is good and does good..."

This blessing was established by the Sages of the *Mishna* led by Rabon Gamliel, in *Yavneh,* after the downfall of *Beitar* (*Brachos* 48b). During this time many Jews were slaughtered and their bodies left to decay in the fields. The Romans forbade the Jews from burying their brethren. The delay of immediate burial was an additional tragedy to the murders, not only because it interferes with the soul's solace but it is a disgrace to the body. This is based on Jewish belief (Avos 4:16) that this world is only a vestibule and the more quickly the body is interred, the quicker the soul begins its true existence in peace. This world is merely the place where we prepare for the World to Come.

> This world is merely the place where we prepare for the World to Come.

Many years later, the Romans finally gave burial permission and the Jews were grateful to Hashem for this benefit. However, as they went to bury the dead, they encountered something miraculous. Not one of the bodies had begun to decay! The bodies were as intact as if they had just died that day.

In response to these miracles in Beitar, the Sages composed the following bracha of thanks to be added to the standard formula of the three Torah-ordained blessings of *Birchas Hamazon*:

Hatov veHaMeitiv

הטוב — Who is good — in general and specifically for the

miracle that the bodies did not putrefy.

והמטיב לכל — and Who does good to all — for the miracle that the Jews were allowed to bury their dead.

Why did these miraculous events prompt the institution of a new blessing to be included and said at every *bentching*, for all Jews of every generation? This additional bracha has special meaning during our exile for all time. Until the time of Yavneh, the text of *bentching* was recited when Jews were in their glorious land. We were able to thank Hashem for the food and for our land and to enumerate the many blessings with which Hashem was demonstrating His love for us and His choice of us as His chosen people in an open way. However, after the downfall of Beitar, there were those who felt that Hashem had rejected the Jews as His people. The exile may have been a sign of long-term rejection. The miracles of Beitar, occurring after its downfall, served as a lesson to us for all time — although we may seem to have been defeated and in exile, Hashem is still watching and caring for us as His chosen people (Rav S.R. Hirsch, zt"l).

This blessing therefore stresses our thanks for the past, present, and the future. It is a continuous lesson for all time, that just as Hashem has helped us in the past, He presently helps us in a hidden manner, and He will continue to help us in the future.

In addition, the miracle of the preservation of the bodies after death served to demonstrate a new insight into Hashem's kindness. Not only does Hashem provide us with food to fuel the body and keep us alive in this world, but even after death Hashem nourishes the soul and cares for our body. The goodness of Hashem is unlimited and eternal!

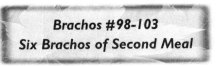

Brachos #98-103
Six Brachos of Second Meal

☙ ☙ ☙

Six brachos will be repeated if we eat a second meal during the day:
1. washing the hands,
2. on bread,
3. on food,
4. for the land,
5. for Yerushalayim,
6. for Hashem's ongoing goodness.

Each time we say these blessings, we can think of new insights to appreciate the words, the lessons and to focus our gratitude to Hashem for everything we enjoy.

Supplementary Blessings

On Shabbos, each Shemoneh Esrei lacks twelve of the blessings. However, the third meal of Shalosh Seudos adds six blessings and the *Musaf* prayer adds another seven blessings. It is suggested that one should eat some extra fruits, sweets and snacks on Shabbos in order to make up the required 100 brachos (*Mishna Berurah* 46:14). One should also listen to the brachos people say over the Torah and *Maftir* and during the repetition of Shemoneh Esrei (to have the merit of these brachos).

There are other ways to accumulate one hundred brachos, such as whenever one uses the bathroom and says the *Asher Yatzar* blessing.

The Rambam concludes his section on *Hilchos Brachos*:

"One should always be careful to avoid making unnecessary blessings but at the same time, one should seek to increase the saying of necessary brachos, as Dovid says, *Every day I will bless You.*"